THE MEMOIRS OF THE HAPPY LESBIAN HOUSEWIFE 2

THE MEMOIRS OF THE HAPPY LESBIAN HOUSEWIFE 2

LORRAINE HOWELL

SAPPHIRE BOOKS

SALINAS, CALIFORNIA

The Memoirs of The Happy Lesbian Housewife 2
Copyright © 2022 by Lorraine Howell. All rights reserved.

ISBN - 978-1-952270-76-5

This is a work of fiction - names, characters, places, and incidents are the product of the author's imagination or are used fictitiously. Any resemblance to actual persons living or dead, business, events or locales is entirely coincidental.

All rights reserved. No part of this publication may be reproduced, distributed, or transmitted in any form or by any means, including photocopying, recording, or other electronic or mechanical methods, without written permission of the publisher.

Editor - Heather Flournoy
Book Design - LJ Reynolds
Cover Design - Fineline Cover Design

Sapphire Books Publishing, LLC
P.O. Box 8142
Salinas, CA 93912
www.sapphirebooks.com

Printed in the United States of America
Second Edition – August 2022

This book is licensed for your personal enjoyment only. This book may not be re-sold or given away to other people. If you would like to share this book with another person, please purchase an additional copy for each recipient. If you're reading this book and did not purchase it, or it was not purchased for your use only, then please return to your favorite book retailer and purchase your own copy. Thank you for respecting the hard work of this author.

This and other Sapphire Books titles can be found at
www.sapphirebooks.com

Dedication

I dedicate this book to my Momma and Daddy who have passed over. They always supported me in everything that I did and I know that they would be proud of what I am doing now. I came out, I am writing which I always wanted to do and I have a good life. That is all they wanted and I have it. Thank you, Mary and Virgil Mason, for giving me the courage to do what I wanted. I love you both.

Acknowledgments

Sapphire Books, Chris and Schileen: Thank you for waiting so long on me while I was having a mini breakdown and having life kick my butt. You were patient and kind and checked in on me and that meant the world to me. I love you ladies.

Leigh Hubbard: Once again, you saw the vision of "The Happy Lesbian Housewife" when she was not looking so good. She is perfect as she is a bit frazzled as all housewives get.

Sweetie: Thank you for being you and allowing me to share our crazy lives with others. I love you!

My precious kids: You allow me to tell the truth about your lives and that means the world to me. You guys are awesome and I love you.

Marianne Furbush: Thank you for staying on my ass about finishing this book. I'm not sure that I would have done so without you.

Introduction

The Big Ole Piss-Poor Pity Party

"Before you diagnose yourself with depression or low self-esteem, first make sure you are not, in fact, just surrounded by assholes."
~ William Gibson

I need to apologize for dropping out of sight for a while. Well, a few years to be honest. Quite simply put, I have been having a big ole piss-poor pity party. Yup, a big ole woe-is-me, thumb-sucking, what-did-I-ever-do pity party! Guess what, it got me nowhere!

I do realize that these past years have been a tough one for so many, and I am no different. I have spent much time thinking about it lately, though. Allowing it to fester and grow and eat at the very core of myself. In the last couple of years, my granddaughter was diagnosed with Tourette's syndrome. My daughter was in an abusive relationship that truly and literally broke parts of her as well as my heart. My youngest son had a facial cyst that filled with infection and turned him into the Creature from the Black Lagoon with its swelling. It had to be surgically removed from his jaw and face quickly before it got very serious and went to his brain. We moved residences, and within a short amount of time, we had to put our beloved

German Shepherd down due to illness just two weeks before Thanksgiving. I had a car wreck a few days after that. I was okay, but the guy that hit me ran and my car needed a thousand bucks of work/tires and that sucked. I got COVID, which lasted for four weeks and made me sicker than I have ever been in my life. That led to me having long-haulers syndrome, which is almost as bad as the actual COVID. Then just a few weeks ago, my dear sweet cousin, who is thirty-six and a single army dad, was diagnosed with Lymphoma that has spread pretty much everywhere. I could go on but it's starting to sound like wah, wah, wah!

    I was feeling pretty sorry for myself. How much worse could this get? What had I done for all of this to pour out on me? Why me? Gloom...woe...adversity. I had a really big old PISS-POOR PITY PARTY! I was basically walking around the house singing the ole *Hee-Haw* ditty about gloom, despair, and agony. Then, this weekend, I was talking to the cousin who had been diagnosed with cancer. He said to me, "Well, Cuz, it could be worse. My feet are healthy. No cancer there!" I kind of sat back and thought a second and, since we had been talking for about two hours, I replied, "And, your tongue seems to work okay too. That's a good thing!" Then we laughed. Hard! Really, really, hard. It was wonderful. His words and humor made me realize that it was time to put on my big-girl panties and get back to knowing that tomorrow would be better and the next day would be even more so! None of this is funny per se, but there is still humor there if you look deeply enough. I also realize that it is not just about me. It is about the lessons I learned and how I learned to apply them day to day.

I am telling you this not for pity, but to let you know that sometimes life gives us shit and it is up to us to pull ourselves up by the bootstraps and shovel our way out of it. We may stink and be a bit tired when we get finished, but we will know that we are stronger and that there is love and laughter under the pile.

Moral of the story: Get the shit out of your own way and get ready for the next year, folks. It's gonna be a doozy! Make it great and remember to laugh. Now, you have a book to read.

Has She Snapped?
~ The Engagement ~

An excerpt from the first book to catch you up. If you've read it, skip on by. If not, WHY THE HELL DIDN'T YOU READ THE FIRST BOOK? Do it. Now. Sheesh!
~ Lorraine Howell (Ha Ha)

Saturday began much the same as the one before. Have I mentioned that I really like to sleep in on the weekends? Or, that Sweetie does not? Surprise! Again, Sweetie once more plopped on the bed at an ungodly hour and lifted my eyelid open. Really? Who does that? And, what is it about closed eyes that is not a dead giveaway that I. AM. SLEEPING?

"Wake up, babe," she whispered loudly. "I have something to talk to you about."

"Can't it wait?" I burbled. "I'm sleeping."

Sweetie was bouncing on the bed. She does not bounce. I grew frightened so I cracked my eyes a bit to see what was going on. That's when I noticed the crazy gleam in her eyes. She had finally snapped. I watch *Snapped* on television a lot. I know all about it. Was I about to die? Then I noticed that she had her hand behind her back. Did it hold a knife? A gun? A blunt object? Shit! Should I try to run? Fight back? Close my eyes and feign sleep—cross that one out. I'd be an easy target if she thought I was sleeping. I sat straight up and faced the giant.

"You can't kill me! You are too smart for this. The first suspect is always the partner. You will never get away with it."

Sweetie looked at me, hand still behind her back, like I was a nutter. Okay, maybe I am. But it was early, I had not had my meds yet and I had watched too much late-night TV. Sue me.

"Kill you? What the fuck are you jabbering about? I'm not going to kill you!" Then she pulled out the ring box.

I gulped and began to tremble again. "Put that back," I screeched. "Gay marriage is not legal in Florida and that was our deal. PUT. IT. BACK!"

Sweetie dropped to one knee right in front of the bed. I covered my head with the bed covers. I must have looked like Jabba the Hutt sitting there like a big lump. I did not care. Sweetie stood, grabbed the covers, and yanked them off my head—which truly did not help my wild morning hair in any way—and went back to her kneeling position.

"Babe," she said sweetly. "I love y—"

"La, La, La, Dee, Da..." I chanted maturely in a singsong voice. I was trembling and had dry mouth. I thought that I had a few months at least. Why was I so freaking scared? I loved this woman. Panic set in again and I began to sweat.

"Hush," Sweetie admonished. "Listen to me. I love you. I want to be with you for the rest of our lives. I never thought the woman that I would say this to would come along, but you have..."

At this point, I noticed that the bedroom window was open. We were two stories up but I am pretty tall, so I figured, "What the hell? It won't hurt too badly." So, I jumped! Straight from our bed. It propelled me sort of like a trampoline, but not. At the very last moment I chickened out, just in time to grab the windowsill with my fingertips.

"Umm, Sweetie, could you help me here? I, err, seem to be hanging from the windowsill," I pled.

Sweetie jumped up, ran to the window, and grabbed my arms. She promised to help me out if, and only if, I listened to her first. I nodded quickly. I'm no fool.

"As I was saying…but you have. So, if you will have me, I would love to be your wife. Will you marry me?"

She then pulled me back in the window, thank God! I looked at the sincerity in her eyes and replayed her words in my head and my heart melted, my sweat and panic flowing away.

"Of course, I'll marry you. Whenever or wherever that may be. I love you with all my heart. I want to be with you forever and that's all that matters."

"So, you don't mind that I proposed to you in the bedroom, in my pajamas, with you hanging halfway out the window?" she queried.

I replied, "Of course not. This is us, Sweetie! I love you and wouldn't have it any other way. At least you didn't have a Breathe Right Strip on your nose."

"HA, HA, very funny, but I love you too." And she placed the ring on my finger.

"So, how 'bout coming back to bed? I think I have a boo-boo from 'falling' out the window and it needs exploration to see if I need stitches or if a bit of TLC will take care of it," I implored with a bat of my lashes.

"Oh, I think I can take care of that baby. Scoot over." She winked.

And They Call It Puppy Love

"New Rule: Gay marriage won't lead to dog marriage. It is not a slippery slope to rampant inter-species coupling. When women got the right to vote, it didn't lead to hamsters voting. No court has extended the equal protection clause to salmon. And for the record, all marriages are 'same sex' marriages. You get married, and every night, it's the same sex."
~ Bill Maher

Wow! So, Republicans have figured me out. I thought I had kept my darkest secrets hidden so well. But apparently, they are all-knowing as they figured out that my secret desire is to marry my pet.

There! I said it out loud! I have loved her for over two years now. She is sweet and shiny and loving and kisses me whenever I am sad. She comforts me and cuddles me anytime I need her. She never asks questions and always agrees with me. She is perfect! Why should I not be allowed to marry my sweet little Miniature Pinscher? Her brown eyes are so very soulful.

That's right, the Republicans figured out that all of my efforts in support of gay marriage were, in fact, a thinly veiled attempt to get one step closer to being able to have my relationship with my adorable pup sanctioned by the church and legally recognized by both state and federal governments.

What idiots! Comparing gay marriage to incest and bestiality—as a well-known republican did in a speech a while back given to journalism students at the College of New Jersey in Ewing, NJ—is just ignorant. Gay marriage hurts no one. These other acts do. Gay marriage is about love, respect, and honor. Incest and bestiality are about power and dominance, not love.

Republicans, I invite you to do your research. Read. Get to know some gay and lesbian couples and their families. Figure out who they are and what they are about, and search your heart for understanding and some love of your own. Stop being so judgmental and learn to live and let live. I will keep you in my prayers. Yep, believe it or not, many gays and lesbians do attend church and pray!

And if I do ever decide to marry my dog, you will be the first on my guest list. We'll be registered at Petco.

Here Comes the Bride

"I love being married. It's so great to find that one special person you want to annoy for the rest of your life."
~ Rita Rudner

Once the engagement anxiety—I mean joy—wore off, Sweetie and I started to talk about wedding plans. I had always wanted a beach wedding, so I told her that and off she went. See, she is a planner that also has OCD, have I mentioned that? Well, she does! She also likes everything perfect. And, well, I just fly by the seat of my pants. Sweetie is also very corporate and I am a hippy-dippy freewheeler. This is not always a great combination when really important things are being considered, like getting married. She pulls at her hair and wheezes a lot. I just grin. Or cry. See, a wee bit difficult.

Sweetie immediately started her research and inundated me with info about all the beaches that we could go to from Florida to Japan. She also researched and overwhelmed me with colors, wedding wear, invitations, blah, blah, blah. I was so overcome by all of this that I had a great idea: we would just elope! That would take care of most of the problems. All that was left was a dress, a suit, flowers, a photographer, a minister, vows, a place, colors, and paperwork... *Sigh.* I plopped to the floor. This was all too much. Why do people put themselves through this? Couldn't a nice little old lady come to the house and pronounce us wives while we wore our shorts and T-shirts? I ran this idea by Sweetie and she just rolled her eyes and went back to her research. She told me to do mine as well and that we would come together and have the perfect wedding. Psssshhh.

As I was doing my "research" (read that as messing around on social media), I came across an article about Women's Week in Provincetown. Well, that sounded promising…and fun. There were women and beaches and comedians and singers and there had to be a minister. What town doesn't have one? I ran upstairs with my find and to my surprise, Sweetie loved it. LOVED IT! What the hell? We agreed on something. Woot, woot!

"Now," she said. "We just need clothing, colors, the perfect self-written vows, and invitations."

"Hey, how about we don't have anyone else there but us? A TRUE elopement. You, me, the minister, and photographer. Sound good?"

"If that's what you want, sure," she replied. See, Sweetie doesn't really like people. So that was a point for me. Also, she had agreed again. Was she possessed, or had she finally gone off the deep end? I didn't care. All I cared about was that, whew, no invitations. One more thing down. Now to move on to the others and see how much I could get rid of.

Travel. That should be next. We wanted to get married on 10/10/10, kinda like 6/6/6, just not all satanical and such. We just wanted a superb day to remember. Or, in my case, an easy day to remember. I forget what I walked into a room for. How was I supposed to remember a date, even one this important?

Sweetie remembers everything. This pisses me off. Oh well, what can I do?

I started the search for the flights. Unfortunately, Women's Week started on the 9th of October and that wouldn't fit any travel plans that I could find. Sweetie did leave that part to me as she hates to fly. I get a kick out of big ole tough her cowering in her seat. I found a flight. Score one for me. It would get us there on the 10th. There went 10/10/10 for our wedding. But I was able to book the flight! That was a positive.

Oh, damn, I forgot somewhere to stay. Back to the computer I went, praying that I could get a room for the night that we were to arrive. Luck was on our side. I found a beautiful bed and breakfast that had a room for our entire stay. Yayyy me! I am so talented.

After doing all this work, I was done. I went upstairs and asked petulantly, "Do we really need our own vows and nice outfits and photographers and colors?"

"Yes," she said with force in her voice.

I knew that voice. There would be no arguing. I was stuck doing more research. Might as well not argue and just get to it. As I mentioned, I am hippy-dippy. I believe in the meanings of colors, stones, and signs. I decided that we would have a handfasting ceremony. I figured that would make her nutty as a fruitcake. Handfasting is an ancient Celtic ritual in which the hands are tied together to symbolize the binding of two lives. The colors have meanings too. I decided that I would pick the colors because I just wanted pretty colors and I would explain them to Sweetie in her terms.

I went to the ribbon store—well, a store that had ribbon—and began with white as the main color.

It means peace, truth, and devotion. That was an excellent start, plus it was a good color to match all the others. Next, I picked light blue for fidelity and longevity. Who doesn't want that in a marriage? Hmm...sounds good. Next came gold because it was mainly pretty. It means prosperity. Yeah, I could get with that one for sure. Green came in immediately after that because it was lying by the gold and I was about through looking at ribbons. It means love and luck. That worked. I searched and searched for pink, because Sweetie hates pink because it is girlie and she is so not. Tee-hee. Pink means love, happiness, and romance. And, finally, I chose black because, believe it or not, it stands for pure love. Also, it was the last spool on the table so there was that. I was done with looking at stupid ribbons even though I do believe in all the hocus-pocus in the ceremony of the handfasting. I went home and showed Sweetie the ribbons and explained the concept to her. To my total surprise, she loved it. Damn, I wanted to make her a wee bit loopy. My plan didn't work. Shit! That was no fun.

Next came the clothing. Oh yay! The following Saturday, Sweetie and I went to the mall. She was able to find a nice suit in short order. I, however, was not able to find a dress, so we had to drag all over town. We went into a high-end store finally, which I did not want to do because I am cheap. Very cheap. El cheapo! But I immediately saw the perfect dress. It was a size smaller than I usually wore but I decided to try it on anyway. I grabbed it while Sweetie wasn't looking and headed to the dressing room. I entered a stall and, whoopee, it fit. I headed out to the open area to get a good look in the three-way mirror and, I'll be damned, there sat Sweetie. I dropped to the floor and let out a guttural yelp while falling to a "poopie in the woods" squat so that she couldn't see how it looked as I tried to crab-crawl back to the dressing room.

"Sweetie, what the hell are you doing out there?" I bellowed. "You're not supposed to see me in my dress before the wedding. It's bad luck!"

"Now who's the OCD planner?" she asked with a snicker.

"Shut up," I spat. "There are rules!"

She left the dressing area due to the fact that I was screeching at her, and I was able to go back out to the area and check myself out. I looked pretty damned good in that dress, and it was on sale, which is my thing. It could have looked like a pilgrim's dress with a big collar and hat and if it had been on sale, I would have taken it.

I carried the dress to the checkout area without Sweetie getting a glance. I paid and got the hell outta there. I was done shopping. It was time to get ready for our wedding. It would start with actually getting to Massachusetts.

The morning of our flight dawned beautifully. I was glowing. Oh, yes, I do know. I saw me in the mirror. Sweetie, however, looked like a frightened skunk. That's a pretty frightful sight. I know. I was looking at her face. It was green. A green skunk. That made me giggle. I got the stink eye for that. Tee-hee...a skunk that stunk. That surely fit. Oh well. Off we went to the airport. Sweetie was becoming different colors as we drove. I was scared that we were going to wreck. I said this out loud. Boy, did I get a look! That gaze could have sent me straight to hell. I grabbed the door handle just in case. We arrived and I was so excited. I was marrying the woman of my dreams and I had tickets to see lots of singers and comedians, including Poppy Champlin and Jennie McNulty. How exciting!

The minute that we boarded the plane, the shit hit the fan. Sweetie grabbed me and loudly whispered, "Let's get off of this plane right now!"

"But, Sweetie, we are going to start our lives together as one…" I started.

"Shut up. I am not flying. There could be a bomb or a loose screw on the wing…"

"Hush, woman," I said all bravely. "Nothing is going to happen. Get in your damn seat."

Sweetie looked at me like I was possessed. Hey, that would have gone with the 6/6/6 wedding date, but I digress. She sat down with a plop and proceeded to grab the arms of the chair with a death grip. She was now white. I was scared. I'd never seen her this way. Drool was running from the right side of her mouth. Her eyes were wide and wild. She was petrified. That's when I began to smile a bit. As we took off down the runway, I grabbed her leg and whispered loudly, "Sweetie, do you hear that rattle? Is it the wing… the engine? What could it be? Are we going to crash before we even leave the ground?"

"Hush, woman, this is bad enough without your cutesy shit," she forced out between clenched teeth. I grinned widely.

The rest of the flight went fine…for me. Sweetie, not so much. She went pallid with every bump. I was a sweet little wifey-to-be and held her hand with each jolt. I will admit that I was smirking the entire time, though. I had found something that I was better at than Sweetie: flying. That was my thing. When we touched down and after Sweetie had drunk about eight of the little bottles of whiskey that you can buy on the plane, we walked...well, she staggered...off and headed to get our rental car via taxi.

The car was too good to be true. I drove only because Sweetie was a wee bit shit-faced. Sweetie always drives because she says I drive like an old woman. This is totally not true. I drive safely. We got in and headed to the courthouse to get our paperwork done since it was on the way to P-Town. I slowly started to tremble. You see, I have an abnormal fear of going to jail for any and every thing that I have ever done in my life, good or bad, and I was sure that the judge at the courthouse would throw me in the clink for a totally made-up reason. Sweetie was the one who was drunk. Why should I go to jail? It should be her for showing up tipsy. When we arrived, a very nice-seeming representative came out to us, took our paperwork, looked us dead in the eyes, and said, "I am not sure about this paperwork. We will see what the judge says. He's pretty tough. I'm not sure that he will sign off on this particular paperwork." My trembling got worse as he walked off. He was going to tell the judge some weird thing like I looked like a serial killer or, in my younger years, I probably did some underage drinking. One of these is true. I'll leave which one to your imagination.

I began quivering in a corner of the room with tears running down my face. I was going to jail for filing the papers to get married, I just knew it. After what seemed like hours, but was probably only ten minutes, the representative came back and looked at us very seriously. He said, "After much deliberation and going back and forth with the fine folks of our court, the judge has decided to grant you the rights and privileges to marry in the lovely township of Provincetown."

He clapped us on the back and said, "Had ya going there for a while, didn't I?" Then he chuckled as he practically skipped off. Jerk! He was having fun at our expense. Who did he think he was?

But I now knew that I was not going to jail. I fainted in relief. Sweetie woke me by smacking my face. Hard. "Get up. You are so overreacting. Why the hell would you go to jail for wanting to get married? Now get your ass off the floor and let's go find a photographer, a place to get married, and a minister. We have three days. Move it, sister." I jumped up in relief. I was safe from the horrors of jail. I wouldn't do well there. I'm too much of a wuss.

Off we went to our bed and breakfast. We didn't even get lost. Just drove straight there. This was because Sweetie was driving now. Her mind has a built-in GPS. I need a navigation system for everything.

The inn was lovely outside. I sure hoped it had a phone book so I could make all the calls that I needed to. As we walked in, I was in awe. It was better inside than it was outside. We had a view of a courtyard full of flowers and an incredible phone book! I grabbed that sucker up and started to look for a female minister. I don't know why it needed to be a female. It just felt right. I grabbed out my phone and started dialing all the lady ministers that I could find a number for.

Meanwhile, Sweetie was left to carry in all the luggage. I got The Look. Don't judge. You know you have given or gotten The Look before. It's scary as hell, but I would not be deterred. I was on a mission. I had a minister to find. I called about 3,982 before I finally found one that was free on the date of our wedding, which had to be on 10/13/10. How was I ever going to remember that date? It had no rhyme nor reason. Sheesh. Also, at some point, our anniversary would fall on Friday the thirteenth. How bad does that suck?

With the minister settled, I began work on the photographer. Luckily, I found one right off the bat who would do the work free if I would mention her name in my book. I recall the name Nancy. That's all. No last name in the recesses of my mind. Look her up. She should be easy to find. Nancy in Provincetown. Remember that if you need a photographer. She's great!

Since Sweetie now had all the luggage in the room and the clothing put up...hey, phone calls take a lot of time. We set out to find a beach to get married on. After getting lost about twelve times we saw the perfect beach, and by that, I mean a beach that had a sign that led us straight to it. It was heavenly. It had water and sand. That did it for me.

With all the important things taken care of, we headed to town to see some of the shows. First up was a famous singer that I will not mention by name as she was obviously...umm...on a "higher" plane. She played the piano with her head. No joke! And said words that didn't match with the melody. Everyone noticed, but not everyone got the giggles like I did. I laughed and sniggered until Sweetie pinched my leg. HARD. That only made me laugh harder. Sweetie looked horrified and grabbed my arm and tried to drag me out of there. But, seriously, y'all, who plays the piano with her head? Maybe if you were good at it...okay. She was not. Her voice was off as well. I'm not one to judge as I can't carry a tune, but she was bad! She is usually so good too. Oh well, we all have those nights. I just wish we hadn't had to pay for it.

That sucked.

After the show—yes, we stayed because we paid for the entertainment and I'm cheap—we headed to an Italian restaurant in town. We were starved. Italian is one of our favorites. How fun. Not! We got there and looked at the menu. There were raisins in the meatballs. Raisins! What the hell? Who does that? We ordered them anyway as we were dying of hunger. Again, RAISINS! YUCK! Never, ever eat raisins in your meatballs. You will not be happy. We ate with a lot of picking out of the fruit. We then headed, gagging, back to our room, where we fell asleep immediately in hopes of getting the taste out of our mouth.

The next morning dawned beautifully...except we both had tiny pieces of raisins left in our teeth. We fought each other for the right to brush our teeth in the bathroom. Sweetie won. I grabbed my toothbrush, slathered toothpaste on it, and ran out to the garden to brush. No way that I was waiting any longer than I had to, and that damned Sweetie had claimed the bathroom first. Once I got all the raisins out of my teeth and gagged quite a bit, I headed back into the room. Sweetie was lying on the bed. She was green again. I was beginning to think that might become her permanent color and I wasn't sure how I felt about marrying a Martian, but I loved her so I guessed that I could live with it.

"Hun, are you ready to head out to find my flowers?" I asked. See, I had remembered. It was a banner day! Well, this task was harder than we thought. No one had flowers. I had my heart set on lilies and daisies. Neither were anywhere to be found. We went to every florist in the town, and there were a lot. I suppose that lots of lesbians must get married in

Provincetown. Well, duh, Lorraine!

Roses, tulips, orchids. Those were everywhere. Not a single lily or daisy to be found. What was one to do? The local grocery store! They always carried flowers.

We found the tiniest grocery store that one has ever seen and in we went. Right there in the front of the store was a single bunch of daisies. I grabbed that bouquet of suckers and ran for the cashier. I had found part of my bouquet. Woot, woot! Now to find a lily. Just one was all that I needed. Sweetie paid for the daisies and off on our search we went again.

We rode and rode until I saw a landscaping store. "SWEETIE, STOP! It's a landscaping store. Maybe they will have lilies," I yelped.

Sweetie slammed on the brakes of the rental car. She wasn't quite used to them, I guess. Either that or my screeching scared her to death. It was probably my bellowing. Whatever. She stopped.

She pulled in and I jumped out of the car before it stopped rolling. I was determined. I ran in and yelled at the poor man behind the counter, "DO YOU HAVE LILIES?"

"Umm, yes, we have three left," he said in a panic-stricken voice. Clearly, he thought I was out of my mind.

"But they have lilies," I declared with glee. "We've done it, Sweetie. We've found my flowers." With that, we headed back to the bed and breakfast.

I used a pearl flower handle to put my bouquet together and stuck them in a glass of water while praying they lived until the nuptials.

That left us the rest of the afternoon to explore. Provincetown is lovely. We decided to go on a whale watching tour. It was fabulous except that a pod of whales obviously thought we were a really huge shark that was there to kill them and they surrounded us and bumped our boat which wasn't up to code, I'm sure. I thought this was exciting and began to take pictures of everything, including the lady puking over the side of the railing. Sweetie grabbed my arm (she was really awfully grabby on this trip) and told me to "STOP! NOW!"

"But I want pictures of everything, Sweetie. Don't you want all these memories?" I asked.

"I WANT TO LIVE," she screeched.

"Oh, they are just little whales. Look at them. They are so friendly. I think they are just escorting our boat on the best route."

"Are you kidding me? That's what you think? Really? They are trying to sink this boat and kill us," she said while hyperventilating a tad.

When had Sweetie gotten to be such a chicken? I stopped snapping pictures to think about that. That's when we got a huge bump and Sweetie went to her knees. All I could think was, "What fun!" as the boat rocked back and forth.

The whales took that minute to gather into their pod and swim away. Damn, I wanted more pictures. I glanced down at Sweetie, and a look of pure relief had washed over her face. "We are going to live to make our wedding. How delightful," she said with what I felt was a wee bit of sarcasm. I took her picture crawling off the deck. I wanted to remember everything about our trip. She was not amused.

The rest of the trip went off without a hitch. Sweetie came around and really enjoyed the whales... from a distance. And, we got some great pictures of the whales, birds, each other, and a few unsuspecting passengers that were picking their noses or wedgies out of their butts. Fun times.

The boat headed back, docked, and Sweetie and I headed to our first comedy show. It was Jennie McNulty. She was hilarious. She did not try to play the piano with her head, but her jokes were fabulous. If you get a chance, go see her. You can ask her if she knows Nancy if you need a photographer. Maybe she will remember her last name. She is in P-Town a lot and knows lots of people. (Look, Nancy! I got your name in here again. I rock!)

When the show was over, we ate at the famous Lobster Pot. I am not a seafood fan, but it was awesome. So much better than the meatballs with raisins. We meandered around town for a while until we saw two men with beards down to their bellies, tank tops, and shorts hitched under their bellies. One was spitting tobacco into the street. It was just like being in *Deliverance.* I was looking for the banjos when Sweetie pinched me under my arm and told me to, "Stop. NOW!"

If I kept getting pinched and smacked and such, I was going to be black and blue for my wedding. We ran away from the guys even though I was trying to tell Sweetie that they couldn't be guys from the place where *Deliverance* was filmed. They were holding hands. They were gay too. It was all good. She did not believe me, and we ran back to our bed and breakfast, leaving our car parked in town for some reason. It would have been so much easier to just drive. Sweetie had lost it. That was a long run, dammit.

Sweetie plopped on the bed as soon as we got back to our room. "Whew, we are safe."

"Sweetie, why did we run back here and leave our car in town? It could get stol..." I started.

"Fuck! The car. We have to go back. Someone could steal it."

"I kinda just said that," I uttered.

"Shut up and let's go!"

Well, rude. Then it hit me. There had been no sex on this trip. And, from the looks of it, there would be none tonight as we were doing marathons instead. What is a wedding trip without sex? So, I got up my courage to ask, "Hey, Sweetie, ya know, we haven't had sex since we got here, and a woman has needs..."

"This woman needs to find her rental car and get it back to the room and sleep. Got it?"

"Sheesh, are we just a wee bit touchy there?" I asked as we raced into town. "Oh, look, hun, there is Poppy Champlin. We are going to see her show tomorrow. Let's go introduce ourselves."

"NO! She will think we are weirdo stalkers..."

I didn't hear the rest as I was already approaching Poppy. "Hi, Poppy. My name is Lorraine and I am the Happy Lesbian Housewife and I am so glad to meet you."

She smiled at me in a very panic-stricken way. "Hi..."

Sweetie caught up to us at that point, grabbed my arm (there came another bruise!), and stammered, "Umm...I'm sorry...we lost our car and she's a bit worried about it and, well, we gotta go!"

"But, Sweetie, I want to get to know Poppy and she's right here." I looked back to talk some more and saw Poppy running down the street. Fast. Hmm... wonder if she forgot her car too.

Sweetie held my hand hard. I thought it was

romantic until she said, "You're not getting away again."

"But there is Jennie McNulty leaving her show. She knows me. Let's—"

"Not just no, but hell no. Let's get the car and get back to the room."

"For sex? Some boot bumpin', bow-chicka-wow-wow," I inquired sexily.

"No. For some godforsaken rest."

I looked at her dejectedly and replied, "But Sweetie…"

She hissed. I hushed. We made it to our car and drove back in silence. By the time I made it out of the vehicle and into our room, I heard light snoring coming from the bed. She was still in her clothes. Well, hell. She was serious. No nookie tonight. I changed and crawled UNDER the covers and slept.

The next day was spent making sure that everything was ready for our wedding. I was very excited. Also, I was sure that there would be sex tonight. I was excited about that too. It had been days. A girl's got needs, ya know. (And there was need. Lots of it. Don't be a hater!)

The thirteenth (look, I remembered the day. Woot, woot!) dawned beautifully. The sun was high and the wind was blowing gently. My flowers were still alive. This was going to be the best wedding ever. I began to fix my hair and makeup while Sweetie sat outside and smoked so she wouldn't see me. The photographer, Nancy (Gotcha in here again. Yay me!), was to be there in an hour to get pictures of me getting in my dress and some before pictures of Sweetie and me. The time flew. Soon, pictures were being snapped by Nancy ⊠ and we were ready to head off to the beach.

The beach was pretty as a picture as we stepped from the car. The wind had picked up quite a bit, though. That's when I noticed our sweet little, and I do mean little, minister. She was so tiny that she was being blown around the sand. Her partner was trying to hold her to the ground. I really mean that she was tiny. And old. Very old. I became nervous. Would this wind break her? That would certainly ruin the wedding...oh, and her life too.

We jumped into place quickly, not even introducing ourselves, and started the wedding. It was wonderful. The wind died down. The minister didn't blow away. Nancy was snapping pictures. Our handfasting ropes were lovely, as were my flowers, and the vows were spot-on. I teared up. I glanced at Sweetie and could have sworn that I saw a tear in the corner of her eye as well. Perfection.

The ceremony ended quickly, and a car drove by and honked its horn as everyone inside cheered. Sweetie and I raised our hands in excitement. Life was good. Then, I took off running and jumped into the ocean. Sweetie gave me The Look. Don't believe me— there are pictures of the jump and The Look. Nancy took them. Boy, Nancy is going to owe me anniversary pictures too, as much as I have got her name in here. I'll just have to find her. If any of y'all do, will you Facebook me with her information? Thanks.

We signed all of our paperwork, hugged, and left the beach. I was wasting no time. We had heard of a little BBQ restaurant in town called Pig in the Poke, I think. Maybe. Well, I was not really sure of the name but a girl has priorities. And BBQ was one of mine! We changed clothing and drove out for our first night's dinner as wives. And we drove, and drove, and drove some more. It was nowhere to be found and by this time we were starving. We could find no restaurants anywhere, so we stopped at the tiny grocery store again and bought a chicken dinner, some paper plates, plastic forks and spoons, and two packs of Reese's cups. Then we went back to the inn and had a delicious deli chicken dinner while sitting on the bed. Then we finished up with the Reese's for dessert and got ready for bed.

Now, don't forget, this WAS our wedding night. Sexy time it was. Until we fell asleep, about fifteen minutes after we got started. This wedding shit was hard, and we were older than we used to be. Sleep is important, so we made the best of it. Aaaah, married life!

The Way to Her Heart Is Pancakes...

"I don't have to tell you I love you. I fed you pancakes."
~ Kathleen Flinn

Sweetie and I have been on a low-cal, low-fat, low-cholesterol diet for a while now. We have been doing so well, but the other night while waiting on the newest TV singing show to come on, we were both craving something; and by something, I mean something with calories, fat, and cholesterol! Sweetie was staring into the refrigerator longingly and I was contemplating any and every thing in the cupboards. She wanted chocolate cake, of course, and I wanted chips, my favorite. But we had cleaned the house of any of the things that could sabotage us...or so we thought! Out of the corner of my eye, I spotted a half-empty box of pancake mix. Oh, happy day!

I yelled out, "I want pancakes!" while holding the box above my head and doing a happy dance.

"Yes," she cried. "Pancakes!"

Then the guilt set in.

"Oh, honey, we can't have pancakes. You have to go back to the doctor and I need to take care of you and..."

"But I *want* pancakes now," she pouted. "You said it and you made me want it."

Well, I hate to see a grown woman pout, even though I, myself, do it quite often, so I looked at the box to check the calorie count...not bad! I checked the cholesterol...again, not too bad...

"Yes, baby," I said. "I will fix you the pancakes."

"Oh, thank you," she said. "Thank you, thank you, thank you!"

"Anything for you, honey," I replied, eyeing the picture on the box, hungry.

So, cook pancakes I did! I fixed a big stack of them and set them out on the plates, poured the skim milk for Sweetie—she IS still watching her cholesterol, after all—and served them to her with a flourish.

She took a bite of her stack of delicious, calorie-laden pancakes, looked at me with love in her eyes, and said, "Damn, baby! I just fell in love with you all over again."

Now, isn't that romantic?

Honey, There's A Train In The Bedroom!

"And she did not have to ask if this was right, no one had to tell her, because this could not have been more right or perfect."
~ Patricia Highsmith

I am preparing to go out of the country for two weeks. I am very excited to be visiting my kiddos! I am not, however, thrilled about leaving my Sweetie! Nor is she thrilled to have me going for that long.

We are still in the, "I'll miss you!" "I'll miss you more." "No, I'll miss you more, baby," "No, Sweetie, I love you. I'll miss you MOST." "But I LOVE you most, so I'll miss you the most!" stage.

Yeah, yeah, I know… EWWWW, YUCK, GROSS…we are a wee bit sickening! We know it. We do not care. So there!

I am leaving on Thursday, so this past weekend was just for me and Sweetie. We cuddled on the couch and watched movies on Friday night. Then we went to bed rather early and planned to sleep very late…if you get my drift. WINK, WINK.

Saturday morning we slept in, which we rarely do, then I got up and fixed chocolate muffins for my Sweetie's breakfast…then we went back to bed…but not to sleep. POW! This continued throughout the day. I felt like a teenager, and a randy one at that! She would walk by, slap my butt, and ZING! off to bed we'd go! I would walk by, breathe in her direction while heading down to do laundry, and KAPOW! sex on the ottoman in the basement! The dogs would bark and we'd go to the dining room to look out the sliders to see what was going on and BAM! sex on the table! The wind would blow and WHOOSH! sex on the stairs! Nothing or nowhere was safe. BOFFO!

After a long and exhausting day, we went back to bed and watched a movie while snuggling and talking. After a while, things started to heat up again. KABLAM! I had forgotten that this could happen this much in one day...I had forgotten that I ever wanted it to. I am not sure that I ever did! But SHAZAM! This rocked! All of a sudden, I felt Sweetie start to shake...hard...really, really hard! ZAP! This really is most excellent! Then I heard laughter. Very, very boisterous laughter. She was rocking and shaking and hooting and still carrying on with what we were doing. BUZZZzzzz...kill. I stopped. SPLAT! ...and asked, "What's so funny?"

She was laughing so hard by then that she could hardly breathe. She shook like there was an earthquake directly underneath our bed. RUMBLE.

"YOU," she spat out between breaths. "You are what's so funny!"

KERPLUNK. "Excuse me," I said. "What'd I do?"

"You don't know?" She giggled. "Didn't you hear yourself?"

"Well, no, I wasn't exactly listening to myself. I was a wee bit busy!" I was a little mortified but started to giggle a bit myself because Sweetie just could not stop chortling and I catch the giggles really easily.

"As you finished," she asked, still chuckling, "You screamed WHOOO WHOOO! You sounded like a train tearing through the bedroom."

The laughter started again. I joined in! We snorted until tears were streaming down our faces. We held each other. We made train noises. "WHOOO, WHOOO...Choo, Choo, Choo, Choo...WHOOO, WHOOO!" We whooped harder. Her naked butt fell off the bed and I had to clutch to keep her from SPLATTING to the floor. We guffawed!

She looked at me, still laughing and with tears streaming down her face, and declared, "Oh, honey, I am going to miss you so much!"

"I love you and I'll definitely miss you the most, Sweetie," I professed.

"But I love you more," she said.

"Just kiss me," I responded. "WHOOO, WHOOO!"

Educational TV

"Life imitates art and art imitates life until both imitate imitation - Reality TV."
~ Brian Spellman

Sweetie and I love both reality and educational television. We actually became a couple by watching a season of *Survivor*. Don't laugh. You can really get to know another person by seeing if they pull for the "good guy" or the "bad guy," like to "blindside" people by lying to their face and then voting them off, or if they would eat sea slugs mixed with urine "for the good of the team." It can really show you who they are...inside! Anyhoo, we love all things reality including *The Biggest Loser, America's Got Talent, The Amazing Race*, and anything on HGTV. We also love educational television like The History Channel, Discovery, TLC and, again, anything on HGTV! Imagine our joy when, while lying in bed a few nights ago, we found a very educational and entertaining reality television show.

We were lying together, flipping through the channels trying to find something to watch before going to sleep. Suddenly, there it was: a show about fetishes. How educational! It actually showed us how other people live out their fantasies and fetishes in day-to-day life. There was a girl who was a fire dancer and boy, could she dance! She belonged to a group that did fire dancing sex shows. Did you know there was such a thing? See, educational, right? They danced while putting fire in strangely intriguing yet equally gross places, then had sex while twirling fire around themselves. Sweetie and I watched in horror/fascination and decided that while fire did seem a bit sexy, we did not have a fire fantasy/fetish. Burning flesh is not sexy to me...and Sweetie does not like to smell yucky stuff—and I am sure burning flesh would smell a bit yucky!

Next up in fantasy land were folks who wanted to dress like and be treated like babies. Now, I do not judge...but it ain't happening here! These folks really were treated like babies while dressed in diapers and booties and such. They peed in the diapers, ate mashed-up food, and talked baby talk. Their "mommies" changed them, spanked them, and took them for walks...IN PUBLIC. Then they would have sex while remaining in baby/mommy roles. Wow... who knew? Again, educational, huh? Sweetie and I decided that this was definitely not for us. I am not peeing in nor wearing a diaper. Sweetie said "Gross, babe" while watching, so I assume that she is with me on the whole diaper thing. Again, no judgment, just a personal choice.

This led to a talk about whether or not Sweetie or I had a fantasy/fetish. I freely admit to a fantasy of fooling around in a public place, not necessarily "doing it" in front of people...just, you know...aaaah well I guess it is all about the "getting caught" aspect. Sweetie told me, "Good luck with that." So, I am thinking this is not a fantasy of hers! Oh well...

All this talk led to some touching and kissing and talking some more. The TV got turned off, the talking stopped, the touching grew more frantic, then Sweetie said, "Oh, God, baby you smell so good!"

Damn, I thought. *She's about to tell me that I smell like butter crackers again. GREAT!*

She snuggled closer, pushed her face into my neck as far as she could, and sniffed so deeply that I thought it would cause her to pass out or hyperventilate or something.

Again, "You smell SOOO good!"

"I know, honey, I smell like butter crackers, right?" I asked before she could say it.

"No, you smell like my pillow" she purred.

"WOW…your pillow. Really? Do you really mean that?" I asked.

"Well, umm…yeah…but…umm," she stammered.

"SHUT UP AND COME HERE," I demanded, grabbing her and pulling her close. Sweetie's pillow is her most favorite thing—except me, of course. "That is the sweetest thing anyone has ever said to me!"

"Huh…umm…you're not mad?" she asked in disbelief.

"No, I know how much your pillow means to you. It's certainly better than some other things I could think of smelling like." I told her. "Now grab those candy booby tassels and your lighter, baby, and let's get freaky!"

We Got Your REAL L Word Right Here!

"Same-sex marriage has not created problems for religious institutions; religious institutions have created problems for same-sex marriage."
~ DaShanne Stokes

Sweetie and I were in the pool over the weekend and the subject of *The Real L Word* came up. The conversation led to us living out our "Real Lesbian Life" for the day and then comparing it to *The Real L Word* once we watched it that night. Compare the two and see which you live each day. Which life is really real in the grand scheme of things? I'll just bet you come to the same conclusion that we did.

Our Day as Real Lesbians...

7:00 a.m. ~ Sweetie wakes up to take the dogs out to potty. She lets me sleep in as she does some computer work on a project that she has due the next day.

8:15 a.m. ~ Sweetie walks back and forth in the bedroom and mumbles about starving to death at any moment if she does not get breakfast. I ignore her as much as possible. The bed feels too good to worry about food.

8:30 a.m. ~ Sweetie does a giant frog leap onto the bed. "Hun, are you awake?" she asks

"No, dear, I am not," I reply.

"But, babe, I'm hungry."

"Then eat."

"But I want your pancakes. You know that I love your pancakes. They are the best. Please, baby..." she says with lots of well-placed kisses.

9:00 a.m. ~ I serve sweetie her pancakes. YES, I said serve. I serve her much of the time. I like it. She likes it. And besides, I am a sucker for well-placed kisses. We talk about what we have to do this day.

"Don't forget that we have to go to the mall today. You have to have new black pants and you really need a haircut because you have that wake tomorrow after work," I tell her.

"Do we really have to go? You know I hate the mall. I'd rather order my pants," she says.

"It is too late to order your pants. You need them tomorrow, so just get ready and don't grumble. I'll clean the kitchen and feed the dogs while you shower. Go on now." I head to the kitchen.

10:00 a.m. ~ I walk back into the living room. Sweetie is watching *Eye for an Eye* starring Sally Field and Kiefer Sutherland on Showtime. She is not wet. She has not showered. "What are you doing?" I ask.

"Watching a movie," she says.

"Why?"

"Because it is a good movie and it came on and I got interested and I was going to shower but this grabbed my attention and I will shower in just a second and come sit with me because I want to hold you for a few minutes..." she blurts in one breath.

"You're full of crap." I laugh. "You don't want

to hold me. You just want to watch this movie and not think about having to go to the mall."

"I love you," she says.

I sat down to watch Kiefer terrorize Sally and her family. I'm easy.

11:20 a.m. ~ Sweetie gets up to shower.

"Where are you going," I ask. "The movie isn't over yet."

"I've seen it before. I'm going to shower and then watch the end."

"HUH?" She is already gone. I stay there to finish the show. I am invested now.

11:50 a.m. ~ Sweetie rejoins me for the killing scene. She goes to dry her hair. I head off to shower and get dressed.

Nothing worth allowing cameras into our life so others could watch so far...

1:00 p.m. ~ We head to the mall. Sweetie puts it off just a little while longer by announcing that she is hungry and that we should eat. I suggest the food court in the mall. She gags. We drive around in literal circles looking for a restaurant that catches her eye. We both know that she is just putting off the inevitable.

"Chili's?" I ask.

"No."

"California Pizza Kitchen?"

"Pizza last night."

"Smokey Bones?"

"Too heavy."

"Panera Bread is all that is left out here. If you don't want that, we will have to eat in the food court," I say impatiently.

"Panera Bread it is."

Finally.

2:00 p.m. ~ We head to the dreaded mall. I am smiling. Sweetie looks like she is going in front of a firing squad. She buys her pants at Dillard's, so we park there and head in.

"It's hot," she says.

"Yes, and we still have to go inside and buy pants."

"But I want to go home."

I leave her in my wake. She follows dejectedly.

My eyes are caught by the lingerie section. "OOOOOOH purple. I love purple. Look at the fit and the lace. That's gorgeous and it's on sale." Sales are good!

"Whattya need that for? It'll just come off." Her mood is not improving.

"What about you go find your pants and I'll do my thing and we'll meet by the escalator when we finish?" I suggest.

"Fine," she says. "It is 2:15. Meet me at the escalators at 2:30."

"You have got to be kidding," I say unbelievingly.

"Nope, see ya then." And, she was gone.

Whoopee. Fifteen whole minutes. I run through the store grabbing stuff, then rush to the dressing room. "Nope. Not a chance. Yuck. Gotta go on a diet," I say as I try each thing on in a hurry. I hurry over to the register and buy my purple lingerie, which I will save for a special evening. An evening when the air conditioning is working well.

2:38 p.m. ~ Sweetie walks up to me at the escalator. She is late. HA!

"There was a line," she says. "Can we go home

now?"

"You need your hair trimmed. Come on now."

2:45 p.m. ~ We find a place to cut my Sweetie's hair. The whole place is run by Drill Sergeant Dyke (D.S.D). Very cute haircut, though. She is giving orders and doing it in style. Sweetie looks rather scared. There are several people in front of her, so she says to D.S.D., "I'll come back in half an hour."

"NO. DON'T GO ANYWHERE. I'LL GET YOU DONE RIGHT AWAY," D.S.D. shouts.

I giggle and whisper to Sweetie, "How sweet, she is helping a *sistah* out."

She shoves me toward the door and tells me that she will meet me in thirty minutes. She does not see the humor in the situation.

As I head out the door I hear, "SO IS YOUR GIRL OUT HERE SPENDING ALL OF YOUR MONEY?" I glance back just in time to see D.S.D. shove Sweetie into a chair. She is the one that will be cutting Sweetie's hair. She is a talker. Sweetie is not. She has a trendy haircut. Sweetie is conservative. I laugh so hard that I almost pee myself. There is a God!

I walk into J.C. Penney, right by the salon. I find a cute white tank, pay for it, and head out the door to find NY & Company.

3:00 p.m. ~ I run slap into Sweetie coming out of the salon. She grabs my arm and hisses, "Let's go. Now." She looks terrified.

"What's wrong?" I ask.

"Hush. Let's go."

"Did she hit on you," I ask, laughing.

"NO. Be quiet."

"But—"

She jumps in. "She cut my whole head in under

fifteen minutes. She said I have a waxy buildup. You will probably have to fix me up. Surely it is not even. She was throwing hair everywhere."

"There, there. It'll be okay. Let me look." I am giggling again.

"Don't touch my hair right here," she almost shouts. She never actually shouts. She almost does this time. I think she is traumatized. I snigger some more.

"When we get home, I will pour Sprite on your hair. That breaks down the waxy buildup. I learned that in cosmetology school," I say.

"Not a chance in hell," she replies.

We stop by NY & Company and I buy a couple of tank tops that are on clearance. As I said, I like a sale.

3:15 p.m. ~ We head home. Sweetie needs rest. Trauma takes a lot out of a girl. A whole hour at the mall, a haircut from D.S.D., and waxy buildup. This is all too much for my love.

Still not a thing worth filming so that others could watch us on TV so far...

3:25 p.m. ~ "Oh yeah, we need spaghetti sauce and toilet paper," I say.

"Just shoot me."

"Don't be so dramatic," I admonish. "There's a Target. We can get it in there and I can pee. I really have to pee, Sweetie."

She whips the truck into Target on two wheels a la James Bond. I grab the "Oh shit" handle and squeal. We go in, she grabs random stuff and throws it in the buggy, and I go pee.

3:45 p.m. ~ We head home for real this time.

Seriously, would you watch us on TV?

4:00 p.m. ~ We pull up to our house. As we pull in, Sweetie admires the greenness and symmetry of our yard, as she always does. I do not notice, I never do. We are "Home Sweet Home." Or, in our case, "Home Hot Home." Our A/C has been acting up. It is hot in South Florida. Very hot. It is miserable. We carry everything inside and put it up. We are sweating. I grab Sweetie and shove her head under the faucet. I then commence to pour Sprite on her hair and work it through.

"Let's go swimming," I say.

She runs upstairs, throws on her trunks and T-shirt, and flies by me. She is out the door and in the water before I can even move. I can't find my suit, so I grab an old pair of her trunks and a beater and go to join her. She takes one look at me in her trunks and the beater and her eyes darken. She likes me in her clothes. I jump in and we make out until Piper, our 110-pound German Shepherd jumps into the pool and heads right toward me. She likes to swim with me and hang around my neck like a big ole baby. Sexy time is over. Mommy-time has commenced. Sweetie grabs a noodle and lies back on it.

"*The Real L Word* starts tonight. Whattya think? Are we gonna watch it or not?" I ask.

"Well, is it like a real, real show with plots and everything, or is it a reality show or a scripted reality show," she asks while trying to balance standing up on the noodle.

"From what I read, it is not a 'show' like *The L Word* was. It is a reality show that follows a group of Los Angeles lesbians. It will follow all the 'pretty people' as they go from club to club or premiere to premiere. And, yes, I am positive that some of it will be scripted as all reality shows are scripted in one way or another," I answer. My son has done a reality show so I know that most all are scripted to some degree.

"But what makes these people interesting enough to watch week to week?" Sweetie wants to know. "Hey, can you stand on a noodle? I can't do it."

"I don't know. Throw the purple one over here and let me try," I say as I send Piper back to the steps of the pool. "I guess it is the fact that they are in LA and they probably have lots of money and they go to premieres and really cool clubs and probably all weigh twelve pounds and are strikingly gorgeous and sleep around a lot. Look, babe, I can do it. I can balance on the noodle."

"How the hell are you doing that? I keep falling. Here, try two noodles. Can you do that, smarty-pants?" she says, then continues. "But why would people want to watch them any more than they would want to watch us?" Sweetie is certainly just full of questions!

"Because we are trying to balance on pool noodles m'love. People would not want to watch us because we are real reality. We are pretty much boring," I answer. "Ta-Da, I can balance on two noodles."

Sweetie takes offense to this. "Excuse me," she says. "We are boring? How are we boring? Why are we boring? Are you bored? Who says that we are b—" She is on a roll.

I jump in. "Hold on, sweet-thang, don't get all crazy. I am not bored. We are not boring in our life, but we are normal. We don't go to clubs. We don't go to premieres. We don't sleep around. Normal and wonderful but really boring to base a television show on. That's all."

"But you said we're boring," she pouts. "I don't want you to be bored. Damn this noodle."

"Arrrgggghhh, I am not bored. Spread your legs a little more. That makes it easier to stand on the noodle," I tell her. "We live our life and I love it. But, Sweetie, think about it. Think about what we did today and what we will do tonight. Seriously, who in their right mind would want to watch it?"

"I can't do it. I just can't balance on the noodle. I am more buoyant than you, I think. Can you make the number three with both hands?" she asked, then continued. "So, we'll finish out the day in our normal fashion then we'll watch *The Real L Word* and see which is more entertaining. Sound good?"

"Yep. Sounds good as long as you won't pout anymore. Of course I can make the number three with both hands. Why?" I ask while holding up both hands with my first three fingers up and my pinkie and thumb touching.

"I can't do that either," she laments. "Look." She holds up her left hand. Perfect number three. She holds up her right. It looks like a lobster claw. Her thumb does not touch her pinkie at all. Her ring finger is crooked downward. The bird finger is a bit low too.

"Damn, babe, what's wrong with it? I hope it's nothing serious. That is your 'good hand,' you know," I say wickedly while wiggling my eyebrows up and down.

"Stop it," she says while trying to make it work. She cannot do it.

"Sweetie, do you really think anyone in their right mind would want to watch us on TV?" I blow on my noodle and send water splashing right in her face.

I giggle. She does not. She turns her back to me. A huge splat of water hits me right square in the mouth. She has blown on her noodle too. The war is on. Piper joins in and we all splash laughingly around for a good while, while the other two dogs frolic around outside the pool, keeping dry.

Still not sure there is anything others would find worth watching on Showtime…

6:15 p.m. ~ We decided to get out of the pool. We go in and I run a bath while feeding the dogs. Then, while I bathe, Sweetie starts dinner. I get out and finish up the pasta while she showers. We have a perfect tag-team routine going. Sweetie then dries her hair. It shines beautifully. The Sprite worked. HA!

7:00 p.m. ~ We eat dinner while watching *The Phantom* on SyFy. And then, during a commercial as we clean up, I say something stupid. A disagreement ensues. Sweetie uses her "serious voice." I cannot stand her "serious voice." It is hot, we are tired, and it gets ugly. Not loud, not mean, just ugly. Feelings get hurt. I get up and go to the bedroom, where we now have a nice wall-mounted TV, and turn on *The Phantom* there.

8:00 p.m. ~ I call my daddy to wish him a happy Father's Day. He is not a big talker. It is a family game to see who can keep him on the phone the longest. I hold the record so far: 22 minutes and 37 seconds. I hope to break it today. He is about to have a nervous breakdown as I keep thinking of something new to talk about. "So, how's the weather?" "What did you do today?" "Have you painted the porch?" "Is blue still your favorite color?" I do not break the record. I keep him on the phone for only 13:48. One of my kids is going to break my record someday. I can feel it.

8:30 p.m. ~ I go downstairs and ask Sweetie if she wants me to make her the dessert that I had planned for her. I have Molten Chocolate cake. I cut a slice.

"Yes, please," she says. "Are you gonna watch *The L Word* with me?"

"I don't know. I am a bit sleepy." My feelings are still hurt.

I bring her the cake and I sit down on the couch to eat mine as well. I watched her as she ate from the corner of my eye. Damn, I love this woman.

9:00 p.m. ~ We sit stoically and watch the beginning of *The Phantom, Part II*. I hate silence. Cricket, the smaller Shepherd, lies down beside me and Juno, the Min-Pin, crawls into my lap. Piper rests at my feet. They know that I am sad. Such sweet girls.

I am sure there is none of this that others would want to watch…

9:45 p.m. ~ "Honey, can we go lay in the bed and watch *The Real L Word* together?" Sweetie asks. "I am taping *The Phantom* and we can watch the last hour tomorrow."

"Okay, if you want," I mutter, and we head off up the stairs.

10:00 p.m. ~ We lie side by side on the bed staring at the television.

After about ten minutes Sweetie mutters, "Stupid."

"Pretty much what I expected," I say.

Another few minutes pass.

"She's scary-ugly," she says about one of the

girls that is particularly skinny.

"Yup," I reply.

More time goes by.

"Boring" she says.

"Kinda," I say. "Should we just turn it off?'

"Yeah," she replies, grabbing the remote.

"Why did what I said bother you so much?" I ask.

"I don't know, but it did," she replies.

"I didn't mean to hurt you. I did not want today to be ruined. I'm sorry."

"Me too," she says and turns away from me onto her side.

Silence.

10:48 p.m. ~ I get up and go down to the spare bedroom to read the new *People Magazine*. Have I said how much I hate silence?

11:15 p.m. ~ I snuggle up to Juno, who jumped into the bed with me. She licks my face. She knows I hate to sleep alone. I get lonely.

11:30 p.m. ~ I head back upstairs. I touch Sweetie on the back. "I love you so much," I whisper softly.

"I love you too. Very much," she says drowsily.

We sleep.

We are not perfect. We act silly. We laugh. We fight. We love a lot. Maybe no one would want to watch our life on television but that is okay with us. The ladies on **The Real L Word** *were pretty boring themselves, and I did not see nearly as much love in their houses as we have in our home. I know that I prefer the life we have, and I believe that Sweetie does too. The ladies of* **The Real L Word** *can have their reality. This is ours, and it's damn good!*

The Rainbow Bridge

"If there are no dogs in heaven, then when I die, I want to go where they went."
~ Will Rogers

Since writing the last book, Cricket, Juno, Piper, and Max have all crossed the Rainbow Bridge. Though there are some stories about them included in this book, we have since adopted two wonderful dogs into our family. They are Mr. Bubby and Charlie. You will also be reading about their escapades. If you have animals that have also crossed the Rainbow Bridge, know that they will all greet us there someday, and Sweetie's and my thoughts are with you.

Hello, My Name Is Max And I Have A Problem

"If animals could speak, the dog would be a blundering outspoken fellow; but the cat would have the rare grace of never saying a word too much."
~ Mark Twain

Upon returning home from a trip to Canada, I was immediately faced with a huge dilemma. My sweet boy had a problem. It had been building for a while, slowly, slowly getting worse. Sweetie and I had tried to ignore it, had spoken with him about it, and had even discussed a medical intervention for him. When I came home the problem had exacerbated to a point where I felt that it was finally time to move forward with getting help for him before it was too late.

"Max," I said with the Mommy voice that said I was serious but supportive. "It's time. Go out to the car, buckle up, and we are going to get you some help for your plight."

He said nothing. He simply dropped his head and did as he was told. We headed out immediately. I drove him to the arranged meeting place and let him out. He headed in without question. He was ready too; I could feel it! I was so proud of him. I parked the

Jeep and headed in to stand in the back of the room for support if needed. I knew I had to let him do this himself, but I am a mom!

He was sitting in a chair on the right side of the semicircle that was to be his support group. He listened quietly as each of the others introduced themselves and shared why they were there. Finally, I saw him breathe deeply, and I knew that he had gathered his wits and was going to finally open up! My heart skipped a beat. I held my breath. The waiting was intense.

He looked back at me, turned to the group, and purred sweetly, "Hello, my name is Max, and I have a problem."

"Hello, Max," the rest of the felines purred.

Max continued with some shame. "I peed on the upstairs hall carpet."

"MEOWWWW," the others purred in support.

"I have not always done it. I don't even want to do it. I just get so angry and strike back in the only way I know how." He moaned.

"Tell it, Max," one especially pretty Manx said.

"It all started with those new pups. The Mommas brought them home unexpectedly. For the longest, it was me and my best friend Tita. Tita was wonderful... for a dog. She was my pet! I loved her! When Mommy came to live with Momma, Tita, and me, she brought Juno. Juno was a trial at first. She barked too much and she took time away from Mommy sometimes. She was also too damned active and drove me crazy..."

"Speak it!" said a Tabby sitting to Max's left.

"But I got used to her eventually," Max continued. "Then the puppies came. Oh my God! They were awful! They still are. I just don't know how to deal with their shenanigans. Then, when our sweet dog Tita died, everything just got worse! So, I began to pee on the carpet in the upstairs hall."

"Let it out," said a gorgeous Abyssinian.

"The puppies bark at me and chase me. They eat my food, Juno especially, and won't even let me walk across the living room without attacking me. Piper sees me walk toward the office and barks loudly so that everyone knows where I am. Cats are supposed to be able to be stealthy...she ruins that! Also, everyone else in the house is female. There are five of them and just one little ole me. That is just too much estrogen for one poor guy!"

"ROWWWWRRRR," the others said in anger.

"The one that they call Cricket puts my whole head in her mouth." Max was gathering speed now. "She tries to chew my ears off. I tried to get the Mommas to understand, but they just love those big ole dumb dogs so much! So, I started peeing on the carpet and then...I even started making myself throw up on that carpet as well. The Mommas were just assuming that I was eating too much, but in reality, I'm forcing myself to barf just to get attention!"

"Oh, purrrrr baby," the Manx said.

I was shocked by this admission. Tears were flowing. I had not realized how hard all of this had been on poor Max. I wanted to pick him up and chuck him under his double chin and tell him that all would be okay, but he was on a roll so I let him continue.

"Now, Momma has had to rip up the carpet in the upstairs hall because it smelled bad..."

Aha, that explains all the mess in the living room and upstairs...but more on that later!

"...and she was grumbling about sending me to

an 'old kitties' home' and I am not even that old—I'm only seven. I'm just pissed off. Everything has changed. Tita is gone! That little yappy dog, Juno, lives here now. Cricket and Piper are too big, and they act like they run the place. Do they not realize that I am in charge? Everyone knows that cats are much more intelligent that dumb ole dogs. EVERYONE!"

"Amen!" said the other mousers.

"I had to get the Mommas' attention. So, I did what I had to do. Does anyone even get that?" he meowed out loudly.

The other pussies wiped their eyes. I could not help myself. I ran over to Max and grabbed him up. "I am so sorry that we did not get how much the dogs bother you. You are an important part of the family. We all love you, Max! You will stay with us as long as you live. I will talk to Momma. You will never have to go to an old kitties' home. Please forgive us!"

"It's okay, Mommy. I understand that humans make mistakes. Just keep those big ole dumb dogs in check and everything will be okay now," Max purred

"Of course, Max, anything you need," I assured him.

As we left the room, I felt him looking back toward his new friends. He winked slyly.

I stroked his back, feeling such relief. He would be okay. Our household would go back to normal. Life was good again...well except for the mess that was now our living room and upstairs hallway.

"Purrrr-fect," said the leader of the group. "She fell for his sob story. We did our job! He will once again rule that household. When will humans realize that not only are we smarter than dogs, we are also smarter than them? Stupid humans."

The group twittered.

"Yeah," purred the Tabby. "So, who is next on our list? Should we help the Persian that is gnawing her fur out because of the new bird in her home, or the Balinese that is eating the fluff out of the pillows because he hates the new baby that his family just brought home?"

"The Balinese definitely," the leader said. "Now, everyone, raise a paw to Max!"

"Here's to Max," the group cheered. "May he once again show everyone that CATS RULE!"

Mariachi Karaoke

"I've been embarrassing myself since about birth."
~ Phil Lester

Sweetie and I decided to go out on Sunday afternoon just to spend a few hours by ourselves. She was so sweet when she asked me that there was no way that I could turn her down. She looked at me as I was straightening the house and said "Hey, I'm hungry, woman. Want to go get something to eat?"

Like I said, she was so sweet that I couldn't turn her down. "Sure, let's go grab a bite, Sweetie. It'll be fun to eat a meal without dog hair in it." We ran upstairs to shower and get dressed, then headed out the door. We got into her truck because she ALWAYS has to drive and pulled into traffic. Then the games began.

"So, honey, where would you like to eat today?" Sweetie asked.

"I'm not sure, Sweetie. What would you like to eat?" I replied.

"It doesn't matter to me. I am not in the mood for anything in particular."

"Me neither," I said.

"Well, honey, you have been in the house all week. So, it is important to me that we go somewhere that you would like to go. So, where is that?"

"I would like to go wherever you would like to go," I shot back, playing our usual game.

"AAARRGGHHH," she yelped. "I will turn this truck right around and we will eat peanut butter and jelly if you don't tell me what you want."

My phone rang then, saving me from a lunch of PB&J I am sure. It was my daughter. I told her that we were going to eat and she immediately said, 'OOOOH, you must try Margarita's. It is delicious.'"

Ding, ding, ding! Ladies, we have a winner. Margarita's it is! I thanked the daughter immensely and hung up.

We were very close to Margarita's, so Sweetie was okay with eating there. We pulled in, got out, and headed up to the door. Right before we were to enter, Sweetie said, "Oh, babe, look right there. How cool is that?"

Well, it was not cool at all. It was gross. It was a pig roasting on a stick right in front of the restaurant. Yuck. The worst part was I could see its eyeball! "Gross," I said. "Are we SURE we want to eat here?"

"Yep," Sweetie replied. "I think this is a good place."

"Well, goody for you. I disagree. There is a pig right there looking at me."

"Oh, honey, just don't look. You don't have to eat it or anything," she assured me as we sat down.

The waiter came over to take our order. Sweetie looked at him with a gleam in her eye and said, "Tell us about your fresh pork specials."

I ran for the bathroom, gagging. When I came back, Sweetie had ordered for both of us. I prayed that there would be no pork. She sat there across from me grinning. She got me. I admit it. But paybacks are hell.

I hope she realized that.

Then I heard it. My chance at redemption. It came in the form of a Mariachi band. Sweetie does not like to be the center of attention. She does not like others to pay attention to her. She hates karaoke and bands that play at your table, so now was my chance. I am not shy. I like music and dancing and being the center of attention. I turned to catch the Mariachi band's attention.

"TURN AROUND," Sweetie hissed at me. "Do not dare get them over here."

"Huh?" I replied innocently. "I am just watching the provided entertainment. Aren't they fabulous?"

"I said DO NOT get them over here," she replied.

"But, honey, listen. They are playing the Elmo song. C'mon, Sweetie, sing with me."

Sweetie's eyes started to change as the Mariachi band began to move toward our table. She gave the evil eye first to me and then the band. Her evil eye is scary. I have seen her frighten off huge angry mobs with that look. But I was on a roll.

"*Bawk-bawk-bawk-bawk*," I continued with the Mariachi band.

"SHHHHHH," she hissed. "I mean it."

Closer and closer the band got to us. The music changed to "It's a Small World." You have never really heard "It's a Small World" until you have heard it sung by a Mariachi band. I joined in. Sweetie glowered. The band was now at the table right behind us. I was dancing and laughing along with everyone else in the restaurant. Sweetie, not so much.

"Play something we know," the man at the table behind us said.

"Aaaah, Mariachi Karaoke," the band leader

said. "Everybody sing with us now!"

Woot, woot... "The Macarena!" I can sing that one too. I can also do the dance. I glanced at Sweetie. There was fire coming from her eyeballs. I stood up to dance anyway. Then I noticed the members of the Mariachi band starting to slink away. They would not make eye contact with us. The evil eye! That is what did it. Sweetie's evil eye was scaring them off.

"Come back," I pleaded. "Please let me dance the Macarena. Let me sing. Please come back to our table."

The band glanced over their shoulders at me, then took off in a dead run. "Está señora loca con mal de ojo," I heard one of them say. I think they called Sweetie a crazy lady with evil eyes or something like that.

"Don't mess with the best, honey. I'll beat you every time," Sweetie announced triumphantly.

"Ahhh, just shut up and eat your pork," I pouted.

A Totally True Text Message
The Roach

Buddy: I just had the biggest roach in my house, Mom.
Me: Really?
Buddy: YES! It tried to kill me. It attacked me when I was at my weakest.
Buddy: (Sent picture of roach) Zoom in on that bitch.
Me: OMG, grab Papa's knife.
Buddy: Did you zoom in on it?
Me: Yes, Buddy.
Buddy: I think it's a vampire. It flew straight at my throat.
Me: It's a water bug.
Buddy: NO! Rish.
Buddy: Damn autocorrect – I mean roach. It stared at me straight in my eyes.
Me: Did it hypnotize you?
Buddy: No, but it tried.
Buddy: I stripped to my boxers. It tried to kill me.
Me: Why strip?
Buddy: So, I knew for certain it wasn't on me… or was on me. Oh, Momma, I was so scared. I still am.
Me: AAAAH, Makes sense. Did you get it?
Buddy: Finally
Me: Glad you prevailed.
Buddy: It was close. I was almost seriously almost

injured.

Buddy: To reach it with the spray, I had to stand on top of the railing on top of the stairs. It was on top of the ceiling. I sprayed it with roach spray and it flew right at me. I jumped off the railing; luckily with no injury.

Me: Did you curse at it?

Buddy: As I was stripping, I did. I am still in my boxers.

Buddy: When it flew for me, I saw my life flash before my very eyes. I wobbled on the railing...the roach flying straight for my eyes. I was praying all the time. It was flying straight for my neck just like Dracula would. I screamed like a little bitch, ducked under the attack, jumped off the railing then cried in the corner while Ansley tracked the monster like the Zulu warrior that she is. She gets it from her family.

Me: Good that you had her around.

Buddy: She's my hero. She saved my life.

Me: This is going in my next book. LOL!

Buddy: Don't laugh Mom. This was serious. And, book, schmook...I'm safe now.

Me: LOL! LOL!

Buddy: Shut up. I am traumatized.

Me: Aww, poor baby.

Buddy: You just don't get it.... :-p.

Me: Yes, yes, I do and it's funny as hell to think of you huddled in the corner while Ansley tracks the poor little roach.

Buddy: IT WASN'T LITTLE! It was a giant and I don't like bugs...oh forget it Mom. You don't understand...

Me: HA, HA, HA, HA, HA!

Buddy: Shut up.

The Zombie Bear A-poop-colypse

"And now I've got to explain the smell that was in there before I went in there. Does that ever happen to you? It's not your fault. You've held your breath, you just wanna get out, and now you open the door and you have to explain, 'Oh! Listen, there's an odor in there and I didn't do it. It's bad.'"
~ Ellen DeGeneres

My dear oldest son, Bubba, posted something on Facebook about a certain brand of cute little sugarless gummy bears. The post began with, "My face hurts..." (from laughing, I assumed). I love me a good giggle so, of course, I followed the link. The stories of what these poor innocent adorable little bears did to your intestinal tract were hilarious, but the more that I read, the more I thought that the reviewers were just trying to one-up the previous one. Thus, the gauntlet was thrown down. I figured that I needed to try these adorable little innocent bears. They looked harmless enough. And really, I've loved anything gummy since I was in high school. What could it hurt? Also, the fact that they were sugar-free practically made them healthy, right? So, off to the store I headed.

I had to look at several stores before I found these innocuous little gummies. I finally entered a drug store, went to the candy aisle, and (insert music and a spotlight here) Ta-Da! There they were. I grabbed up a couple of bags and was on my way. I headed home to begin my experiment.

When I pulled in, Sweetie's car was there. Oh joy, maybe she would try them too. I went in the house and immediately told Sweetie what I was doing and that she was free to join me. I showed her the reviews and she simply glared at me and said something about her now knowing for sure that I was batshit crazy. I was not to be deterred, though. I would prove all those reviews and Sweetie wrong. Hrrrumph!

I tend to think that I am a pretty smart woman and have a pretty high tolerance for most things, so I ate approximately fifty of those cute little buggers. Sweetie watched me with narrowed eyes and a twitch as she continued to read the reviews. She then rolled her eyes as I was popping those little bears into my mouth, one after the other. I guess some of the said reviews were fairly colorful. Whatever! This was my body and my bears.

I put on my pajamas and sat down to watch TV. I felt fine for an hour or so…then suddenly something evil rolled in my tummy. I thought that I had just eaten too many of the damned bears. Next, something akin to a grenade detonated in my lower intestines. I curled into the fetal position and waddled at a fast clip, with my butt cheeks clenched tightly, to the bathroom. What the hell? Were all those people right? If the stuff spewing in cresting waves from my rear end was any indication, they did not lie.

Sweetie said with a chortle, "Oh, hun, are you okay?"

I couldn't answer her as I got up and shuffled back to the sofa just as a wave of gas hit me. I figured if I just let a little gas out, all would be well. WRONG! Oh, my Gawd, the stench of the gas was worthy of blaming on the dogs. Then I felt it, another grenade way down deep. I got up and ambled slowly to the bathroom—AGAIN—and was hit with the walking farts. And, they weren't little toots, either. They were lumberjack farts from the pits of hell. I was dying. I was sure of it. My colon was splitting apart. To prove that point, I then sharted. How becoming of a lady.

When the next wave hit, I used the furniture for support. The pain was horrendous. Just as I was almost to my bowl of safety, it hit. I was going to poop in my pants and there was nothing that I could do about it. I cocked my leg a tiny bit and was pleased to find that it was just another series of foul, reeking, house-clearing farts. Sheesh, the stench was unbearable. The smell caused my eyes to water. The dogs whimpered and ran for cover with their tails between their legs, and Sweetie wisely said, "Well, I guess you should have believed the reviews, and by the way, you stink." She is so very helpful! NOT!

Puddles of sweat on my whole body began dripping down my aching frame. Another wave of cramps hit my belly like an erupting volcano. There were rumblings, grumbles, roars, and the threat of another eruption of hot lava much like Mt. Etna—which has been erupting for 3500 years. A scream escaped my lips, and I did the best run that I could do while clenching my ass cheeks in my hands and being bent like Quasimodo. As I finally sat down on my beloved toilet, I realized that the gaseous fog that I had created in the bathroom made it tough to even see the shower. What the hell? Another abdominal-twisting, shriek-inducing ripple of pain started at my belly button and traveled through my entire intestinal region. With a final growl, my anus sent a message to my brain. "Hey, I know what you did and that I am about to be torn to shreds, but what can we do now? You shouldn't have ever eaten those evil bears." Geez, even my sphincter was smarter than me. With a final scream from the pits of my gut, the volcanic material shot out at Mach speed. My bowels were spewing out all of the evil not only in my body, but all the evil in the world as well. Molten lava hit the bottom and sides of the toilet with the force of a small bomb. It was as if everything that I had ever eaten or even smelled blew out at once.

"Sweetie, I think I just shat my colon," I yelped. "Sweetie…Sweetie…" She had deserted me, or at least the gaseous stench that was permeating our home. "Sweetie, I need some of the baby wipes that we have for Steven to wipe my butt. Dammit, Sweetie, answer me!" I was crying by this time.

I got up and, clenching the cheeks of my butt together, shuffled slowly over to the dresser where the wipes were. I grabbed them up and kissed them. My butt couldn't take any more toilet paper. After cleaning myself, I just lay down on the bathroom floor waiting for the next wave of diarrhea, of which there were seven. Somewhere in there I started to giggle. I always giggle at the most absurd times and things. This brought on another round of farting. I laughed louder.

Sweetie, who had been outside, peeked in and wailed, "Holy shit, woman, what is wrong with you? Why are you giggling?"

"Shit…ha, ha. My shit made me giggle. Those reviews were correct. I am officially an idiot."

Sweetie nodded in agreement.

"Thanks, Sweetie. I love you too!" I replied sarcastically.

Once I was finally able to pull myself up and drag myself to the kitchen, I asked Sweetie if she wanted a cherry water, because I'm helpful like that. She did. I put some of those frigging bears in hot water to melt them, then added the bear juice and the cherry packet to a bottle of water and shook it hard so that there was no trace of said gummy fricking bears. Sweetie has to go to work in the morning. Ha, ha. Payback's a bitch!

FLASHBACK
And There They Went

"Embarrassment is a villain to be crushed."
~ Robert B. Cialdini

After the birth of my oldest child, Bubba—who was a very large baby, by the way—I needed to go out to buy diapers. To be honest, I really just needed to get away from poopy diapers and breastfeeding for a while. After securing my son and an extra bottle of freshly pumped breastmilk with my parents, I headed to K-Mart to purchase the aforementioned diapers. I had not bounced back to my pre-pregnancy weight as Bubba was only three weeks old, so I wore a comfortable dress, my nursing bra, and a pair of granny panties that I had worn during my pregnancy.

As I drove into the parking lot, I was feeling like a perky teenager again, not the frumpy, frazzled new mom that I surely looked like. I climbed gingerly out of the car, as I was still a bit sore, and headed to the front door. Freedom felt wonderful, if only for a short time. I grabbed a shopping cart and began my shopping trip by sauntering up and down the aisles looking at new clothes that would fit me when I did get back to my previous weight. I then headed to the makeup aisles and had a blast looking at the new fall colors of nail polish and eye shadows. Life was good.

After I picked a beautiful red for my fingernails, I began to feel my granny panties slip just a little. No problem—I just tugged near the waist of my dress to drag those puppies back up. I continued my march of freedom. I was feeling great. I looked up and down the toy aisle thinking of the day my son and I could play with the tiny cars and basketballs. My panties were still slipping a bit and my boobs had started to leak as it was nearing my son's feeding time. Oh well, I was going to make the best out of my little excursion, so I kept going.

As I started to walk down the baby aisle, my panties began to droop lower and lower. I began to walk like a duck to keep them up. My knees began to separate and point outward. The panties slipped lower and lower. What was I supposed to do? My panties were going to fall if I didn't do something, so I squatted down to inch them back up. I was gripping the cart handle with a death hold. Shit! What was I going to do? My panties just would not go up, so I started to wiggle like a stripper on a pole. I bounced and flounced and wiggled round in circles. I would not be defeated by a pair of old lady drawers. To my surprise, I felt them level out. They were not where they should be, but I thought that I could get what I needed and get out before a catastrophe happened.

As I stood back up, my underwear began to slip lower and lower. Dammit all! I began to walk, knees out, like Charlie Chaplin. The panties hit my thighs. I then decided that there was nothing else that I could do except run. I grabbed a pack of diapers and some diaper rash cream and took off...fast! The panties slunk downward farther. A realization hit me. This was not going to end well. I slowed my run and began to saunter so as not to draw attention to myself. The underwear scooched on down. I pulled my knees together in a normal walking fashion…and there they went. I felt them fall to the ground. So I stepped out of them. Right there in the middle of the jewelry aisle. I was done. There was nothing else that I could do. I left them there and began to run with the cart so that no one would see. Surprise—people saw it! They looked at me as if to chastise my panty drop. I stared straight ahead as my boobs started to leak in earnest. Wet stains began to appear on my dress. I was a mess.

I slowed to a normal clip, acted like the panties belonged to someone else, and headed to the checkout lane with people still snickering around me. I held my head high as if I had no idea what was going on. The cashier rang me up while looking at the other patrons giggling at me. I paid, then reached out for my bag and ran like a scalded dog to my car. I just wanted to get home and never leave my house again for fear someone would recognize me. Someone else could get the damn diapers from now on.

Needless to say, I no longer wear underwear.

Traitorous Doggie-Children

"In the whole history of the world there is but one thing that money cannot buy...to wit—the wag of a dog's tail."
~ Josh Billings

As I was making our bed this morning, I heard a strange noise coming from our newly painted downstairs bedroom. I tried to ignore it for a while, but it sounded like someone was up to something in there, and since I thought everyone else was sleeping and Sweetie was at work, I was intrigued. I headed in that direction and there was my sweet darling middle fur daughter Cricket sitting in the center of an entire roll of toilet paper that had been torn methodically from the spool. It spread from the bathroom wall out into the bedroom floor. She still had a piece hanging from her lips and I swear she was grinning. Cricket is our mischievous fur child. She tends to get into things that the other two just don't think of. We expect it now. Like the good mommy that I am, I explained that we did not waste toilet paper because it is not good for the environment as well as being fairly expensive. Cricket just rolled her eyes at me and walked away. I called Sweetie and told her what HER daughter had done. Sweetie just chuckled and said, "Well, at least she had fun." Momma Sweetie does not have to clean up the mess, so it is cute to her. Mommy, however, did have to clean the mess up, and cute? Hmm, not so much.

    I headed back to make the bed and after about fifteen minutes, I heard pounding at the slider door. The girls were wanting to go out to play. That seemed like a great idea. I could get some work done. Down the stairs I headed again. This time it was our youngest fur daughter, Piper, that was leading the charge. I opened the door and all three girls ran out only to stop dead in their tracks due to the oppressive heat. It was like they hit a wall. They turned right around on the patio and ran back into the house. No one wanted to play any longer. I tried to explain that they needed to get out and get some fresh air and sunshine. I assured them that they would not have to be out too long and that they most certainly would not die of heatstroke. They all three looked at each other like I was an idiot and sauntered toward the living room to lay under the vent. I suppose you could say they are a bit spoiled and like the creature comfort of air conditioning. They are much like their Momma this way. She is a bit hedonistic.

    I left them lounging and headed upstairs again to finish up in the bedroom. Ten minutes later, I heard a commotion and some pretty high-pitched screeching. It sounded like someone was slaughtering a hog in the living room. I flew down the stairs. Cricket had Juno, the oldest yet smallest fur daughter, in a headlock. Juno did not seem to appreciate this at all and was wailing her displeasure. I extricated the poor little babe's head from Cricket's hold and enlightened her to the fact that one did not choke their sister, no matter what their sister did. Juno ran off in tears and hid behind the bed. Cricket stuck her tongue out toward Juno's disappearing rump. I started to shake. It was only 9:30 in the morning and I was exhausted.

I sighed and gave up on making the bed. I plopped down on the sofa to start some work on the computer. I hadn't been sitting there long when Juno brought over her favorite toy. She wanted to keep it from her sisters. She shoved it underneath my left butt cheek, tucked it in tight, and smiled happily. No one would find it there. I thought I should have been offended about the reference to my butt size. I was, however, too tired to care so I just left it there and continued my typing. Juno walked off like a queen and blew a raspberry toward the other two girls who were searching for the toy. Good grief. I needed just a few minutes for myself.

I called the girls over and explained to them that Mommy was very tired and that it was time for a nap. They wanted to sleep by me, so I told them that as long as they were quiet they could lie on the couch beside me and rest. They assured me that they would be good. That lasted for about two minutes. That is when the "she's touching me" started. As quick as a wink, I separated them. Cricket lay on my right side, Juno on my left, and Piper behind me. Quiet settled in. I was ecstatic. Finally, I could get some things done. Whew! Hallelujah! Woo hoo! Then, I smelled it. Someone had farted. Not just a little fart. A silent but violent one. It was so bad that it made my eyes water and I threw up a little bit in my mouth.

"Who did this?"

The older girls turned around and glared at Piper. I turned my head slowly to my baby, not believing that anything that bad could come out of someone that sweet. She was clenching her eyes shut pretending to be asleep, but she was snickering. I could see her shoulders shaking.

"Piper, did you do this?" I asked.

She let out a big ole fake snore. The older girls twittered. I banged my head on the keyboard. I was still pounding it when Sweetie walked in at lunchtime.

"Why are you here?" I asked.

"I tried to call you and you didn't answer. I was worried about you and the girls. Where are the girls?" she asked, ignoring the red lump on my forehead.

I looked around. I did not see them. I ran into their room and there they lay, all three of them, sleeping peacefully.

"Oh hun, what sweet girls we have. Just look at them. So quiet. So sweet. So obedient. How did we get so lucky?" Sweetie asked.

I let out a primal yell. I had raised three children of my own, two boys and a girl. It had been easier than this. I know it had. Dogs are much more work than children. Our three canines are proof of that.

"Sweet. Sweet? Oh my God, Cricket ate the toilet paper, Juno says my big butt is as big as a toy chest, and Piper farts like a truck driver—"

"They are good girls, and you know it," Sweetie interrupted. She then gave them each a pat on the head, shook her head at me, and proceeded back to work. Everything was right in her world. She does not live in mine. The girls waited until Momma was gone, high-fived each other, then the two big ones grabbed the bedspread in their chops and started to play "toss the little dog in the air."

I let out a small whimper, kissed each cherubic face, then walked slowly back up to the bedroom and got busy. I am the Mommy after all. That is what I do.

Little dogs stink too! Guest writers, the big dogs, comment...

"Acquiring a dog may be the only opportunity a human ever has to choose a relative."
~ Mordecai Wyatt Johnson

In *Happy Lesbian Housewife: You Can't Make This Stuff Up*, I wrote about our two "stinky dogs." They were very upset with me and asked that they be able to write something. So, without further ado, I introduce you to my guest writers...Piper and Cricket!

In her last book, Mommy told everyone that we were smelly! Well, that may be, but geez, did she have to tell everybody? We are just babies and we get dirty and we do NOT like to go and let other people put their hands all over us. We don't know where their hands have been. Also, at that "smart pet" place that Mommy talked about, they put a noose around your neck! That was scary! But what we really want to talk about today is the little dog that lives with us. She laughed at us when she read Mommy's story. How mean!

The little dog stinks too! Mommy didn't tell you that, but she DOES. Mommy gives her a bath because she is little and doesn't fight very much (because she is dumb and we are smart cuz we went to puppy preschool and graduated and everything) then Mommy sprays smelly stuff all over her. WOW, talk about stinky! Mommy says she smells like vanilla or something but she kind of smells like butter crackers. Momma says Mommy smells like butter crackers too, but Mommy smells good. The little dog does not.

The little dog also wears a pink sweater when she goes outside. HA! A PINK sweater. How dorky. We try and try to bite the pink sweater off so she will look like a real dog (Momma says she is not a real dog) but Mommy yells at us to stop biting her. We are NOT trying to hurt her; we only want to help…most of the time. We know she has short hair and it has been a bit cold here but seriously, a **pink** sweater… just "**DOG UP!**"

Another thing about the little dog that bothers us is that the little dog barks and barks when the Mommas start to go anywhere. We do mean ANYWHERE! Momma says she is a "nutter" and needs medication and that makes Mommy mad sometimes. We are not sure what a "nutter" is, but we think she is crazy! Why ya got to bark like a goof? That is not going to stop the Mommas from leaving and for pets' sake, they are going to come back. The little dog is just a big ole baby!

And ya know what else? When it rains or is really, really cold, that block-headed little dog won't go outside to potty! We guess that she thinks she is going to melt or something. Hrrruummppphh…she is SUCH a princess. She even barks and barks to let the Mommas know if we are eating poop and that makes them holler at us! Why's she such a tattletale? Ole busybody, that's what she is. She also digs ALL the holes in the yard. She does...she really, really does! We have proof...sort of. Well, not really, but it sounded good.

Anyway, we just wanted to let everyone know that we may be a little icky sometimes but it's not all that bad. We just stink like normal dogs that dig in the yard and eat poop. At least we are real dogs—just ask Momma! She knows cuz she knows everything and she says the little dog is really just a rat. So, take that you little butter cracker, pink-sweater-wearin', nutter princess rat! Who's laughing now?

Thanks very much for having us as your guest writers, Mommy!

Piper and Cricket

When asked for a comment about Piper and Cricket's writings, the little dog, Juno, had this to say:

"I will not lower myself to the big dogs' level by commenting on this slanderous drivel. I pride myself on maintaining the highest level of dignity and tact. Therefore, I will simply ignore this piece of fluff as I tend to ignore the big dogs. I must run now and hide all of the big dogs' favorite toys. Have a splendid day!"

—Juno, AKA "the little dog"

What Was That Noise?

"A good fart joke makes me bawl with laughter, so will somebody farting. And the word 'poo.' You can't beat a good poo joke."
~ Jenny Éclair

The first thing that you have to know is that I am very comfortable with bodily functions. Well, clearly not the first thing. I guess after the previous few essays you already know!

I raised two boys and a girl who thought she was a male as a child. They farted at every given chance. You should also know that I find farts and poots funny. I can't help it. I giggle like a seven-year-old boy every single time that someone lets one rip.

Recently I was at the airport and had to go to the bathroom. IT. WAS. FULL! I waited, shifting from foot to foot, for my turn, and when it came up I hopped, holding my crotch, into my stall. As I was peeing, I heard the fart of all farts coming from the stall beside me. I looked up to see if the lady that farted had flown upward through the ceiling. She should have, as it was a blast-off fart. A fart with major hang time. A whoop de doo fart that went on forever. I bit my lip to keep from giggling. The lady in the stall beside me, however, did not. She let out a roar of laughter that could be heard out in the halls of the airport. I'm not talking about a mild, stifled laugh, or a laugh that could possibly pass for choking. She was belly-laughing, crowing like a crazed bird.

I was still covering my giggles so that I would not embarrass the poor farting lady, but it became too much and a loud guffaw blurted from my mouth. So much for being a proper Southern lady. Pssshhh, who was I kidding? I had never been known as a proper lady—or even a lady, for that matter.

My horse-laugh led to every single woman, except the poor pooting lady, (isn't *pooting* a funny word? HA HA!), to begin to chuckle too. The entire bathroom was in a fit of giggles. My stomach was hurting by this point. I was finished with my business but knew I could not get up and leave for fear of being caught as the loudest laugher of all. As I said, I am not proper.

The laughter went on and on, and no one was leaving their stalls so as not to embarrass the poor woman by coming face-to-face with her. How embarrassing. A whoop de doo fart in the public restroom? I just knew that I would stay in my stall until everyone left.

Finally, I got tired of waiting in the stall and was hearing other women start to exit as well, so I got up, still horse-laughing, and opened my door. All of the stalls except one were empty and there was no line. I guess the people in line didn't find the fart funny. Those of us that had exited the stalls washed our hands and laughed harder. We all looked at each other like we would never hear a fart like that again and giggled some more.

The pooter was still locked tight in her stall as we left. Poor thing. I hope she doesn't miss her flight. Oh, who am I kidding? I hope she makes her flight and poots just as loudly in the bathroom on the plane as she did in this bathroom. After all, aren't bathrooms just made to fart in? Yes, they are! Just as farts are made to laugh at.

The Apple Doesn't Fall Far From The Tree

"Love is like a fart. It's warm, unpredictable. And sometimes it stinks, but it can also be the best feeling in the world. That's why I'm so happy that I passed you that day. I know now...I fart you."
~ Ryan Higa

While out doing some shopping with Sweetie, I found the perfect gift for our grandson Steven. It jumped right off the shelf at me and I grabbed it in midair. It was a fart gun. Yippee, what a great present for both the grandson and me. I immediately decided to have some fun with this most fantastic toy. Sweetie saw what I had and just slid down the wall, dropping her head. This was going to embarrass her, and she knew that I didn't care. I was going to have some fun and nothing she could say would deter me.

The store was full of people on this particular Saturday, and poor Sweetie just looked at me with pitiful eyes and said, "Please no, just NO!"

I smiled sheepishly and started to plot out a course of action for maximum amusement. I hid the fart gun, within reach, under a shirt in the cart then headed down the aisle. Sweetie sighed and tried to look like she didn't know me. I just smiled innocently and kept walking. Almost immediately, I saw an older gentleman bent over to look at a water toy. I pulled the trigger on the gun and a loud, obnoxious fart noise came out. The old man jumped up like he'd been shot. I smiled sweetly while holding my nose and sniffling as he grabbed at his butt and looked around with a red face. He then slunk off obviously thinking that somehow, he'd been the guilty party and didn't even feel it. The giggles began to well up inside.

Next up was a harried woman in the book aisle and her three young sons. She was looking at some coloring books and the boys were fighting with some swords that they had picked up. The poor, stressed mom was trying to get the kids to calm down when I pulled the trigger and a single, lingering toot came out. She looked at the boys with irritation and said, "Okay, who did it?"

The boys looked at each other to see who was the guilty party. I pulled the trigger again, and this time it was a long, wet sounding fart. The woman glared as all three boys denied doing the deed. I looked at the poor lady and said, "It's okay. My kids used to do the same thing."

The boys were getting louder and louder as they each tried to blame it on the other. Their mother just grabbed her cart and walked off while murmuring something about "death" and "bringing the boys into the world so she could take them out." The boys were pronouncing their own innocence while trying to blame it on each other. I just giggled and looked for my next target.

Walking down the next aisle was a sweet little older couple. I grabbed at the handle and it let out a quick succession of poots. The sweet lady looked at her husband and said, "Bill, I can't believe that you did that in the store. In the house is one thing, but the store is another!"

"It wasn't me," he protested. "I swear!"

"That was the walking farts, Bill, and you do that at home all the time. I recognize your brand of flatulence. Don't try to place the blame on someone else." She looked at me apologetically then walked over to pat me on the arm. "Please forgive my husband. He does this all the time at our house. I'm sorry if it seemed as if he was laying the blame on you."

"Oh, it's okay. My Sweetie gets the walking farts too. I'm used to it as she always tries to blame it on the dogs," I said with faked sympathy. I smiled at her with understanding and continued back toward Sweetie. I found her hiding behind the bicycles, so I walked up to her, cocked my leg, and pulled the button. The loudest, grossest sound emitted from the gun, and I immediately fanned my rear while Sweetie put her hand to her heart. Everyone was staring at us, and I thought that I had finally gone too far and she may just die.

"Wow, what a relief," I exclaimed loudly while still fanning my butt. "Whoop, that one has hang time doesn't it, Sweetie?"

Sweetie glared at me. I could see death rays spitting from her eyes. I just smiled and said, "It's time to meet Sissy and Steven for lunch. Let's pay for *our*...I mean Steven's...new toy and head on out."

Sweetie followed me to the register waiting for me to "fart" one last time. She was pitiful looking, so I was a good girl and didn't use the gun again. We simply paid and headed to the restaurant for lunch. Sissy and Steven were already there, so I grabbed the bag with the fun new plaything in it and walked toward the door.

We were seated pretty quickly, and my daughter headed off to the restroom. I presented Steven his gift and he was thrilled. He giggled and sniggered as only a four-year-old boy can do. He began to let out low sounds from the gun. As Sissy came back, Steven put his new toy behind his back and "fawted" deafeningly with his gun. He looked at the other patrons in the restaurant and announced at the top of his lungs, "Aaah, I feel all better now!"

I smiled proudly and high-fived him over the supposed "fawt" as Sissy slumped in her seat covering her eyes. The little old lady at the table beside us looked at him sweetly and said, "Don't worry, honey, my husband does that all the time! He gets the silent but violent poots every night."

Steven smiled sweetly and replied, "Oh, my Momma gets those all the time. She is a stinky mommy."

My poor daughter slunk deeper in her seat and rolled her eyes and said, "Thanks for the gift, Mom. Just know that the apple doesn't fall far from the tree. Steven is just like you and Buddy."

She says that like it is a bad thing! MWHAHA-HAHA!

Finding Mr. Bubby

"Dogs are our link to paradise. They don't know evil or jealousy or discontent. To sit with a dog on a hillside on a glorious afternoon is to be back in Eden, where doing nothing was not boring--it was peace."
~ Milan Kundera

Sweetie and I were dog food shopping one day. We had decided that the dogs eat better than us because their food costs more than ours. Anyhoo, when we walked into the pet food store there were several dogs up for adoption. My heart skipped a beat and I looked at Sweetie with puppy dog eyes. (Notice that pun there? Tee-hee!) I grabbed up a cute little dog and looked soulfully at Sweetie.

"NO," she said with authority. "Not a snowball's chance in hell. We have two dogs already and do not need another one."

I pouted a bit but realized that she was right. Two dogs were enough. Then I noticed Sweetie's face. It had fallen. Have you ever seen a face fall? It is quite scary. The skin sags down to the neck and the eyes droop to the mouth. Poor Sweetie looked pitiful. I followed her droopy eyes to a pup in the corner of the cage and saw the most pitiful dog EVER! His eyes were turned to the floor and he was shaking.

"Sweetie," I admonished. "You said no more dogs. Did your droopy face make you forget that already?" I wasn't sure if a droopy face could cause your brain to misfire too, but in this case, I was thinking it had.

"But look at that poor dog. He's shaking and looks so very sad. He needs a good home. Don't you agree?"

"You said no more dogs. You can't just change your mind on me. You know how confused I get," I reminded her.

"Well, that was before I saw Mr. Bubby," she answered.

"Mr. Bubby? You mean you have named him already?" I realized then that it was a done deal. We would have a new dog. Sweetie was smitten.

She and I went over to the adoption people and asked about the pup. The nice lady told us his story. He had been used as a bait dog then dumped in the Everglades when he got too big for the other dogs to want to beat the hell out of him. She also told us all that we would have to go through in order to adopt Mr. Bubby. Home visits, vet calls, yard inspections, a lecture about the pool. Sheesh! It would be easier to adopt a child. A child from another country or even another planet. We scheduled a home visit and walked out with Sweetie smiling from ear to ear...no more droopy face. She had surely done a complete turnaround. I thought, in her eyes, that we had enough dogs. Oh well, I guess there were snowballs in hell. Who knew?

Two weeks later, after all the checks and balances, Mr. Bubby arrived at our house. The poor dog was a wreck. His eyes darted from corner to corner as if he were awaiting a monster or demon to come out and eat him. He had idiopathic seizures where his head shook up and down. For the entire first week, he cowered on the corner of the couch in fear, using the bathroom only when we drug him outside. And I do mean DRUG! He shook and looked around like death was imminent. On about the sixth day, he arose from his corner of the couch and walked over to our very new, very beautiful, and expensive rug, and squatted to pee. Yes, he squatted to pee. He hadn't yet learned to raise his leg to urinate like a big boy. This is a great cause of worry for Sweetie. She thinks that the beatings that he got before we adopted him has made him a wee bit slow. She also thinks that he has short-term memory loss, as when she leaves for work, he does not recognize her when she returns. He barks and barks at her and he has a very scary, loud bark. Also, he hates normal clothing on people. He totally freaks out and barks like a mad dog. He only likes pajamas, or in our case, T-shirts and shorts. He has fits at our regular clothing so we have to change as soon as we get home. I don't mind, though…jammies are much more comfortable, don't you think?

As Mr. Bubby became more acclimated to the house and its other occupants, he started to move around more. One day as I was lying on the sofa for a nap—don't judge…you nap too—I felt dog butt right on my head. I tried to open my eyes but there was a canine penis right in them. GROSS. I had a penis in my eye. I don't want a penis anywhere but especially not in my eye. He was just sitting there licking his no-nuts (he had been neutered). How icky is that? I'll tell you! IT. IS. VERY. ICKY! A penis and yucky no-balls. ACK!

Mr. Bubby continued to sort of get used to his new home. One day he was out in the yard—all by himself, no less! Pretty soon the other dogs joined him, and within minutes I heard squealing. I ran to the slider to find that Mr. Bubby had dug a hole big enough to put Juno, the little dog, in. She was furious and letting the entire neighborhood know it. Sweetie went out and blocked the hole off with screening because she had just put down new grass. Mr. Bubby just looked at her with his big, sweet, soulful eyes and picked up a square of new grass and carried it down to the fence and spit it out. That was a big ole "Fuck you" to Sweetie, don'tcha think?

His next trick was bringing trees in. Not sticks, big ole honking limbs that were bigger than him. He would lay these on the floor and chew on them until bark was everywhere. He chewed faster than I could grab the scraps. Our house looked like a forest.

Through all this, Mr. Bubby was still a frightened dog. He shook and tremored if we said anything too loudly. He still had his seizures. He still sat on the back of the couch. But he was coming along. He was now the man of the house...even though he still squatted to pee just like a little girl.

Shit Happens

"Some people are so positive, that when they slip in dog poop, they pirouette."
~ Josh Stern

Sweetie and I had been out doing our weekend running around and farmers market shopping and had just arrived back home. I opened the door and stepped across the threshold to our living room when the stench hit me. It also hit Sweetie, as I could see her eyes begin to water and her nose to crinkle. "Good Lord, what is that smell?" she bellowed.

"I don't know but it's horrible!" I had pulled up my Denver Broncos shirt and was covering my face with it in order to staunch the stench.

"Oh, my G..." She trailed off to a whisper as a thought hit her. "Do you think it's Bubba?"

My oldest son Bubba was staying with us for a while, and Sweetie was thinking that the stench belonged to him. I glanced around the room and noticed that his door was shut. "It could be, Sweetie. He has been known to clear a room or two in his lifetime."

"That smells like death. Go see if he's okay."

"YOU go see if he's okay. You know that I don't do smells well."

Bubba chose that moment to open his door and walk into the room. He smiled brightly, then suddenly grabbed his nose and said, "What the hell is that smell?"

"I'm not sure, son. We thought it might be you."

"Thanks, Mom! On my best days I can clear a room, but this is a whole-house-clearing smell." He disappeared back to his room and shut the door quickly.

Sweetie and I dragged the fruit and vegetables behind us to the kitchen, still covering our noses. We set everything down and began to walk around, looking and sniffing. The stench permeated every room as we went from the basement to the upstairs bedroom.

"Sweetie," I bellowed from the office. "Do you think the dogs could have done this?"

"No way," she replied from the kitchen.

"Well, what the hell is it then?"

"Oh no. It must be the septic tank." Sweetie ran out the back door at an alarming pace. I hadn't seen her move like that in years. I was impressed.

I grabbed two bottles of air freshener, one for each hand, and began to walk from room to room, spraying everywhere. Sweetie walked back in and said, "Negative on the septic tank."

I was walking around to spray the sofa when suddenly my bare foot hit something very slick and very warm on our beautiful, flowered living room rug. My arms flailed to the side as I hit the floor. I landed hard on my butt and felt the warmth spread up the side of my denim shorts. "OH MY GOD! Help me. I found the smell."

My sweet wife ran straight out the front door. Such a caring woman she is. "Hrrruummppphh!" I thought.

Sweetie peeked around the doorjamb and asked, "What is it? A dead animal...rotten food...what..." She was stammering.

"It's poop. Slimy, wet dog poop." I started gagging. "I'm going to throw up and I can't get off of the floor. Help me, please. I'm dying here."

Mr. Bubby, our newest dog, looked at me with his big eyes and I could see guilt. It was his diarrhea that I was flailing in. The other two dogs had disappeared outside. Even they weren't able to stand the disgusting odor that I was now bathed in.

"Sweetie, get yourself in this house and help me up," I bellowed. "Now!"

I looked around and realized that Sweetie was cuddling Mr. Bubby and telling him "It's okay," and "I'm sorry that you feel bad." Great. I was swimming in poop and she was commiserating with the dog that had dealt it.

Bubba chose this moment to stick his head out of his bedroom door and gales of laughter erupted from his belly. The boy was laughing at me. "Seriously?" I bellowed just as Sweetie erupted in belly laughs.

"What the hell is wrong with you both?" I asked between the bouts of gagging that I was going through. I tried to get up just to slip back down in the mess, rubbing my elbow right through the doggie doo. "Help me now!"

"Oh no," Sweetie answered. "That is rank!" She and Bubba continued to laugh at me. NOT A THING WAS FUNNY ABOUT THIS! Why the hell would they laugh at my misery? Assholes, that's what they were being.

I reached out for the coffee table and pulled myself up to my knees. My legs, arm, and butt were covered in doggie doo. Gross! I crawled out of the yuck and was finally able to stand and run up to my bathroom just in time to throw up. Between barks of laughter, Sweetie called up the stairs, "Are you okay?"

"No, I'm not okay. I'm covered in dog poo and am hanging over the toilet and I can't even get my clothes off and I STIIIIINK," I bellowed.

Whirls of laughter were still heard from downstairs. Jerks! That's what they were. The both of them. Just jerks. I began trying to peel my soiled clothing off of my body and reached in to start the shower. I would ignore the two jokers. That's what I would do. They could kiss my butt. My nasty, dog-crap-covered butt!

After I showered, I put on clean clothes and went to the top of the stairs just in time to see Sweetie roll up our lovely, dog-poop-laden, three-hundred-dollar rug and carry it straight out to the trash. I trailed behind her with my soiled clothing. As we turned and walked back up the porch stairs to continue cleaning and de-smelling the house, a truck came to a quick stop in front of our trash can. A man jumped out and grabbed the rug and threw it in the truck's bed. I glanced at Sweetie and Bubba, who was now standing in the doorway, and we all exploded in raucous laughter.

"Just wait until they get that home." Sweetie giggled.

"Oh well," I answered, chuckling. "Shit happens."

FLASHBACK
Sissy Of The Jungle

"The great thing about having a bunch of kids is that they just remind you that you're the person who takes them to go poop. That's who you are!"
~ Angelina Jolie

Once upon a time, my kids—Bubba, Sissy, and Buddy—and I went on a camping trip. One day we decided to do some hiking. Through the woods we went, happily singing. The kids were sixteen, fifteen, and ten. Life was good.

The young'uns were climbing and frolicking as kids do. I was looking at the beautiful and colorful foliage and listening to the birds and the water in the distance. What a great idea this trek was.

We continued our walk when suddenly we came upon a giant bare tree with a rope tied on it. The rope went out over the water. What fun!

The kids' eyes lit up. They saw the possibilities of a good time. They weren't in their swimsuits and the air was a bit nippy, so they decided to just swing back and forth over the water. The boys went first and were immediately having a blast. The raucous laughter that emitted from them was heartening. I was so happy that they were having fun.

Sissy was whining for her turn, so I got the boys off the rope swing so that she could have it. She was elated. She grasped the dirty rope tightly and clenched her legs around it. Her smile was bright. She jumped up and off she went, flying through the air.

Everything was great until the incoming return. Sissy was coming in at a high rate of speed. I ran to the crest of the hill in order to catch her. I missed. She smashed into a tree. Hard! I rushed to her to make sure that she was okay. She slid down the rope quickly, plopped directly on her butt, and had a really strange look on her face.

The boys were rolling with laughter at the fall. Sissy motioned for me to come over to an out-of-hearing-and-seeing spot in the woods. I slipped away from the still giggling boys. She looked at me with an embarrassed expression on her face and said, "Mom, I think that I pooped in my pants when I hit that tree."

"Excuse me?" I said.

"You heard me," she replied. "I am not repeating it."

"But you must," I said. "I am not sure that I heard you correctly."

"Mom, I think that I pooped on myself when I hit the tree," she hissed through closed teeth. Unfortunately, she did not realize that her brothers were close enough to hear her now, and that her mother could not hold her laughter very well. Gales of laughter took the boys and myself over. Oh, my gosh, was she serious?

She huffed and grabbed my hand to pull me away from Bubba and Buddy. "Will you look, Mom?" she asked with a dead serious tone.

"No! I will not look. It's your poop. You look."

She dropped her pants and panties, and sure enough, there was a perfect turd. She had literally shit her pants! I grasped my sides and cackled—as did the boys, who were hiding (not so well) behind some tall weeds.

"Sissy pooped her pants. Sissy pooped her pants," ten-year-old Buddy sang out.

"Shut your face!" Sissy said with a huff as she pulled up her pants. "Mom, make the boys go away. I have to take care of this."

"Boys, go away. Sissy has to clean the poop out of her panties," I said with a giggle.

"Mother, stop giggling. These are my favorite panties," she whined. They were a lime green pair with a lone daisy on the side. This only served to make me laugh harder.

"Sissy, honey, it's okay. I'm sure that this has happened to lots of people," I said with a snicker as she dug a hole and buried her flowered panties deep in the dirt.

"Oh, shut up, Mom. Stop trying to make me feel better," she said while grabbing up a handful of leaves to clean herself, "It has not happened to lots of people. I am probably the only person in the entire world that it has happened to."

"Yes, Sissy, you are probably right. No one else is as special as you," Bubba said. The boys and I collapsed in laughter as a panty-less Sissy huffed off back toward the campsite.

I smiled wickedly. This would make for jokes for decades to come. Life was indeed good…very, very good.

A Totally True Phone Call
There Is No Mr. Howell

Ringgggg....
Me: Hello
Telemarketer: May I speak with Mr. Howell?
Me: I'm sorry but there is no Mr. Howell here. Can I be of service?
Telemarketer: May I speak with Sweetie Howell?
Me: I'm sorry but she is not here either. She is at work. Can I help you?
Telemarketer: Well, no, I need to speak with Mr. or Mrs. Howell.
Me: Well, legally, I am Mrs. Howell.
Telemarketer: I thought that you said that she was at work.
Me: Sweetie is, but I am Mrs. Howell too. I'm her wife Lorraine.
Telemarketer: How is that possible? There is supposed to be a Mr. and Mrs. Howell. How can there be two Mrs. Howells? Are you sisters?
Me: No genius. As I said before, I am Sweetie's WIFE.
Telemarketer: Huh? Her wife?
Me: Yes, her wife.
Telemarketer: Is that possible...I mean legal...I mean...How...
Me: Yes, it is possible as well as legal. You guys need to update your scripts, because the times, they

are a-changing.
> Telemarketer: Click!
> Me: Tee-hee!

It's The Little Things In Life

"My theory on housework is, if the item doesn't multiply, smell, catch fire, or block the refrigerator door, let it be. No one else cares. Why should you?"
~ Erma Bombeck

Sweetie came home from work one Friday afternoon and she was totally giddy. "It's that time of year, babe. I am so excited!" She then headed up to the bedroom to change. I could hear her. She was whistling. I was scared. And confused.

As Sweetie headed back downstairs, I was scratching my head. *What time of year?* I thought. Had I missed our anniversary...again? Was it someone's birthday? Hell, it could be Thanksgiving or Christmas. I am just not good at keeping up with dates.

"Oh really? That time of year already?" I said. "How exciting!" I was searching my brain to come up with the right "time of the year." I was coming up with a blank.

"Oh babe, I am so glad that you are in this with me this year. You've never been excited about it before. Let's start." She then grabbed two of my gossip rags off of the table and dropped them in a big black trash bag that had magically appeared.

"Wait, I'm reading those. What are you doing?" I asked while grabbing my magazines back out of the bag.

Sweetie just grinned and said, "Free Shredding Day is upon us. We must get all the old papers and mail and tax returns…"

"Free Shredding Day?" I asked incredulously. "What the hell is shredding day?"

"You know, where you take all of the old papers and such to the bank and they put it in a big shredder and shred it all at once so that we don't have to. Shredding Day, babe! It's a big deal." Sweetie was now on a tear, running from room to room gathering up any piece of paper that was not nailed down. I was chasing after her grabbing my bills and scraps of papers that I had written notes on for stories.

"Grab some trash, babe. It will make you feel liberated from the chaos that this garbage causes." She grabbed our Melissa Etheridge tickets off the refrigerator. I snatched them back quickly and shoved them into my bra. Sweetie was actually glowing. I wondered if she was feverish.

This went on for over two hours. I just sat and watched her go from place to place like I was watching a tennis match at Wimbledon.

"Sweetie, we are under a hurricane warning. Matthew is brewing on the coastline, and I am not sure that they will be holding any outdoor activities."

"Shredding day cannot be canceled. It must go on. We need to rid ourselves of this rubbish," she continued.

I grabbed a Macy's catalogue out of the pile. Some things needed to be perused before any "shredding" happens.

"Hey! Put that back. It is trash," Sweetie bellowed and grabbed at the book in my hands.

"No, let it go. I haven't looked at it yet," I said

while pulling back at it.

We pulled and tugged until the catalogue gave way and I plopped backward on my butt. Sweetie was thrilled and added the torn pages back to the ever-growing pile.

I gave up and skulked off upstairs to bed. Sweetie followed suit, still muttering over the importance of shredding day and why didn't I understand.

The sound of wind and rain woke us early. Hurricane Matthew was coming very close and things were decidedly bad outdoors.

"Sweetie, I think shredding day will most likely be canceled. Look outside."

Sweetie got up and looked out and her face fell. She was devastated. I actually felt sorry for her. She *was* really looking forward to Shredding Day.

"Call and see if it's still on, Sweetie. I'll go with you," I said. It was the least that I could do.

"Nooooo. It's called off. I just know it." She looked like a forlorn baby that couldn't find its favorite toy. She wore this same expression until the next Friday, when she started all over again. "Grab that junk mail. Shredding Day has been rescheduled for tomorrow!"

"Oh yay," I said sweetly...or snidely, depending on which of us you asked. I dropped two envelopes in the bag and went off to read. I was NOT doing this again.

Saturday morning dawned very, very early. Sweetie said that we should arrive early to avoid the lines because everyone would be there shredding too. We lugged the huge paper-filled bag and threw it into the back of the truck. Sweetie hopped behind the wheel. She was alarmingly giddy, which worried me a bit. She was so pumped up that I was afraid the top of her head would pop off. I watched to see if it would pop right off because that would be cool.

We arrived at the bank where the shredding was taking place and SURPRISE! No one was there. This confused poor Sweetie. "Where is everyone? Why aren't they lining up in the street? Are we late?"

Sweetie pulled around and took her free token, then headed to her beloved shredder. She handed the token man our coin then insisted that we be able to watch the shredding take place. She stuck her face to the monitor on the shredder trucks. You could see a bit of saliva drool from the corner of her mouth. The look on her face was orgasmic. "Let's go, babe. The free shredding is over for this year." She clapped her hands and did a little jig.

I rolled my eyes until I was looking backward into my brain. I was lost as to how this was fun. I guess, for Sweetie, it's the little things in life.

I'm Dying

"Tis healthy to be sick sometimes."
~ Henry David Thoreau

One lovely Sunday morning, I was awoken by the sweet, dulcet tones of my dear Sweetie. "Oh my God!" she yelped from the bathroom. "What the hell is wrong with me? Honey, get in here right now. I need help. Something bad is wrong."

She then got very quiet. I took that as a sign that everything was okay, so I rolled over to go back to sleep. I drifted back off pretty quickly, as I tend to do. It was the weekend, after all.

"Dammit, babe! Come here. Something is very wrong with me," Sweetie screamed.

I jumped up at the alarm in her voice this time and ran to the bathroom. Sweetie was staring into the mirror with pure horror on her face. "What's wrong?" I said, matching her alarm.

"Just look at me," she said. "Don't you see something terribly wrong with this picture?" she said while waving her hand, Vanna White style, in front of her face.

"No, Sweetie, I don't see anything."

She then thrust her tongue out at me and IT. WAS. BLACK! "What the hell? What did you do to your tongue? Did you break it again?" I was frightened now. When sweetie broke her tongue before, it did not turn colors. AAAAH, come on, ladies, you know that you or someone you love has broken their tongue before. It happens.

"No, I did not break my tongue again," she muttered with irritation dripping from her voice. "Something dire is wrong with me."

"Well, let's go to the doctor, then," I replied.

"I am most certainly not going to the doctor with a black tongue. That is gross and embarrassing."

"Well, what do you want me to do, then?" I asked.

Sweetie began to dance around the bathroom at this point. There was no calming her. This tongue thing was bad. Not just for her, but for me too. *Wink, wink.*

"Dr. Google," I screeched loudly. "Dr. Google will surely be able to diagnose you." I ran to grab the laptop and began a search for "black tongues in humans." Here is what I found, "A black hairy tongue is caused by too much bacteria or yeast growth in the mouth. The bacteria build up on tiny rounded projections called papillae. ...Instead of shedding as they normally do, the papillae start to grow and lengthen, creating hair-like projections. They can grow to fifteen times their normal length."

"Oh, my gosh, Sweetie. It says that the black part of your tongue can grow like hair up to fifteen times their normal length," I told her. "What fun! We can actually braid your tongue hair."

"NO! We can do nothing of the sort. I'm dying and you are making jokes," she shrieked. She was getting good at shrieking, I noted. Sweetie sat down on the bathroom floor and began rocking. She was probably worrying about me actually trying to braid her tongue hair.

"I was not joking. It would be fun to braid a tongue, but there are some more causes," I said helpfully. "Lack of teeth brushing or mouth cleaning, smoking cigarettes or cigars, radiation treatments for cancer to the neck or head areas, ingredients in mouthwash that contain peroxide, menthol, or witch hazel, excessive use of black tea or coffee, lack of saliva or conditions that affect the salivary glands and certain antibiotics that cause yeast overgrowth in the body or mouth."

"I have smoked my whole life, I brush my teeth," she informed me. "And I have never had this happen. I don't drink tea or coffee, so that doesn't make sense either. Read some more."

I was staring at her mouth wondering if I could really braid the black stuff and maybe put beads on it, when her voice snapped me back to reality. "Read, woman! What is your holdup?"

"Well, I was wondering if I could really braid…"

"Stop it. Hell no! YOU. ARE. NOT. TRYING. TO. BRAID…"

"Alright, Sweetie. Don't get your tongue hairs in a bunch." I snorted.

Sweetie fell over in the fetal position. This was more serious than I thought. I poked her and she just moaned. I read on. "Sweetie, here are some more things that cause black tongue: inadequate fluid intake and dehydration, injected street drugs, and it is more often seen in men than women."

"I drink enough water to float a small boat, I don't even take aspirin," she screeched. "And, I am a fucking woman…" Her voice trailed off as the reality that she had something dreadful began to set in.

I continued reading. The next thing I found was "medications that contain bismuth (Pepto-Bismol)." DING, DING, DING!

"Sweetie, did you take Pepto-Bismol last night?"

"Well, yeah, my stomach was acting up. Why?"

"There ya go! That caused your black tongue," I screamed elatedly. I had done it. I diagnosed her and probably saved her life. "Whoop, whoop!" I danced around the bathroom.

"Really? Are you sure? I am not dying?" she whispered as she sat back up.

"No, you are not dying. It says here it will go away all by itself."

"I don't have to go to the doctor or even in public until it goes away?" she asked.

"No, honey, you don't have to go in public," I answered as I headed downstairs.

"Where are you going? I still need you here with me," Sweetie asked

"Well, since you are not dying, I'm gonna go get my beads, baby. Then we're gonna have some good ole braiding fun." I grinned wickedly.

FLASHBACK
Buried Kids

"What strange creatures brothers are!"
~ Jane Austen

My children and I had a nighttime ritual when they were little. I would bring them drinks of water, read them a story, say their prayers, and tuck them in snuggly.

I would then get called back, especially by Buddy, as he was the youngest. There were always shadows on the wall, noises under the bed, monsters in the closet, and scary things everywhere.

One night I read them their chapter of *The Littles* and was talked into another chapter. This was quite normal. I'll admit, I'm a pushover. I sent them all off to their own beds and prepared myself for the ensuing "Momma, there's a monster under my bed." I heard some whispering in the boys' room for about a minute but then there was nothing but silence. Hmmmm…

I enjoyed my good fortune and settled in to read a good book. After about ten minutes of reading, I listened again. Still nothing. Wow, this was a banner night. How could there be no shadows on the walls, no noises in the closet? I began to wonder what was going on. Was one of them strangling the other, or were they just really tired? I read for another fifteen minutes before I got worried. This was unusual.

I got up, laid my book down, and went off in search of the reason for the quietness. First, I checked on Sissy, since she was in a bedroom by herself. She was asleep. Next, I walked toward the boys' room. I heard sniffles as if someone were crying. Uh-oh. I knew it was too good to be true.

I headed to the boys' room and the sniffles grew louder. I walked in and heard snores from Bubba's bed. Then I looked toward five-year-old Buddy's bed. He was sniffling quietly under the covers and tears were rolling down his face.

"What's wrong, Buddy?" I asked quietly so as not to awake the sleeping Bubba.

"Momma, why did you kill your other kids?"

"Excuse me? What other kids? What are you talking about?"

"Your other kids. The ones that talked too much."

I looked toward Bubba's bed. This had him written all over it. He snored LOUDLY! He was trying to convince me that he was sleeping. I called bullshit.

"Bubba," I said loudly. "What did you tell this boy?"

"Shhhh, Momma, be quiet. You'll wake him up and he'll be mad."

"So what?" I said.

"Well, if I cause you to make noise, we'll wake him up and then you'll kill me and bury me in the backyard with all of your other kids."

"Huh? What other kids?"

"Your other kids that made noise."

"Bubba, open your eyes this second and tell me what's going on," I demanded.

"SNORE!"

"You are fooling no one. Open your eyes and

explain, young man!"

Sheepish eyes opened and looked at me guiltily. "Mom, Buddy talks so much and so loud that he keeps me awake every single night, so I told him that you killed your noisy kids and buried them in the backyard."

"You did WHAT?" I bellowed. "You scared your poor brother to death!"

"Death?" Buddy squealed. "Are you going to kill me now?"

"No, Buddy. There will be no killing here. There never was. Bubba told you a fib. I never had any more children. No one is buried in the backyard," I soothed.

"Really?" Buddy asked in a non-believing tone.

"Really," I promised.

"Oh, thanks, Mom. Now he'll jabber all night long."

"Serves you right. I hope he talks the entire evening."

"You won't kill me and bury me, Momma?"

"No, Buddy. As a matter of fact, I think that you should say your ABCs and then count to one hundred tonight in a very loud voice."

"Really?" Buddy asked joyfully. "And, you promise that you won't kill me?"

"Oh, no. As a matter of fact, I'll help you so we can be very, very loud," I replied gleefully.

"Mom," whined Bubba.

"Your brother can join as well if he wants to," I said as we began in a loud tone. "A...B...C...!"

"MOMMMM," yelped Bubba. "That's not fair."

"Oh, you be quiet, Bubba, or I will kill you and bury you in the backyard."

And That Is Why I Shop At A Big Box Store

"Sometimes crying or laughing are the only options left, and laughing feels better right now."
~ Veronica Roth

One lovely Sunday morning, Sweetie and I planned to head out to our local farmers market and meat shop. This place has the best produce and meat in the town. It is a very small store with usually about a thousand people crammed in there. To say the least, Sweetie hated going due to the crowds, but she freely admitted that the cost and freshness made it worth the trip.

It was still early in the morning and I was fully awake and ready to go, which was a miracle in itself. I was feeling kinda cute because I was in my favorite pair of shorts, which I have had for years, and a cute new shirt. We jumped into Sweetie's big ole truck and off we went. We bantered back and forth while we drove. The mood was light. Upon arrival, I jumped out of the truck and was ready to proceed while Sweetie began grumbling about the crowds, which were even heavier than normal. Her eyes narrowed at the denseness of the horde that was milling around.

"Are you sure that you're up to this, Sweetie?" I asked.

"We're already here, so we might as well head in," Sweetie replied with dread in her voice.

I skipped merrily into the throngs of people crowding the store. I *was* feeling kinda cute after all. Sweetie drug along behind me like Quasimodo.

"I have the cart, Sweetie, so you just follow me," I said.

"Do I have a choice?" she muttered back while pulling out the shopping list.

First, we needed some shaved parmesan cheese, so I grabbed some and walked on. Apples were next, and I snatched up several and bagged them up. I bent over the cart to drop them in and felt a little tug in my shorts. Ignoring it, I kept on shopping. I picked up a large watermelon and reached over to put it in the cart and felt a tiny rip close to the pocket of my shorts. This would not dissuade me as I walked to the meat counter. I asked for some chicken breast and filet mignons. I reached up to the counter and felt another tug. Sweetie had walked to the produce section, so I headed over to meet her. People were staring and gesturing at me. I knew I was looking cute in my outfit but really, this was ridiculous. I waved at a few of them to show that I recognized their envious looks.

I caught up to Sweetie and she noticed the crowd behind me as they talked and pointed. "Babe, why are all those people pointing at you?" Sweetie asked from the far end of the shopping cart.

"Probably because they like my new shirt and these shorts. It's a cute outfit, right, Sweetie?"

"Yes, honey, you always look beautiful to me, but those people are sniggering under their breath," Sweetie answered.

Sweetie fought her way through the crowd to see

what all the excitement was about. Suddenly, I felt her slam into my back.

"OOOH, Sweetie, is that a carrot in your pocket or are you just happy to see me?" I said, wiggling my eyebrows up and down. I felt her eyes roll back in her head. "Why are you pushing me along? No one can see my cute outfit if you are jammed into my back like that."

"No," she hissed into my ear. "But they can see your whole left ass cheek."

"What do you mean they can see my ass cheek?" I replied. "I have on my favorite shorts. They are not too short. My ass cheek cannot be showing. They are just jealous."

"No," she said in a mock whisper. "Honey, your ass is showing. Your whole pocket is torn off like a flap and your ass is shining white. This is what you get for not wearing underwear."

"Oh, hell no," I said, embarrassed. "That can't be. These are my favorite shorts."

Sweetie then reached up and grabbed my bare ass cheek with her cold hands and began to giggle. "How do you plan to get out of here?"

"Stand close, Sweetie," I begged. "I have to figure out what to do because we can't walk with you stuck to me like a fly to flypaper. People will stare."

"Babe, they are already staring," she replied with mirth in her tone of voice. "They have all gotten a good look at your butt."

"Oh my god! What do I do?"

"Why don't you head to the truck and let me finish the shopping?" she answered, still giggling a bit.

"How am I supposed to get out of here with my butt hanging out?"

"I don't think it matters, babe. Most of the other shoppers have seen your ass already." She giggled.

"HUSH!" I hissed. "I need to escape with at least some dignity."

"Your dignity fell out the hole in your shorts," She was fully laughing now.

I stood there waiting for just a bit, trying to figure out the best course of action. Finally, it hit me. I would walk out with my head held high and my ass cheek shining. I told this to Sweetie, who just shook her head at me. She was belly-laughing by now.

"You thought they were all pointing and sniggering because you looked cute, and all the while your ass was shini…" She drifted into fits of laughter.

"Shut up," I interrupted while grabbing my purse. I then held my head up high and proceeded toward the entrance, ass bare. I waved at everyone as I walked by and muttered about this being the newest summer fashion. "It's all the rage on the New York runways."

I heard Sweetie whooping from behind me as I headed out the door. "Let her laugh," I muttered under my breath. "Just wait until next time. I will take a damned razor blade to her shorts pocket and show her."

People in the parking lot began to stare and point as well. I finally grabbed for my pocket, which was flapping in the wind, and ran like a scalded dog to the truck. I jumped through the door toward safety. My cheeks were now flaming. This, my friends, is why I now do all my shopping at a big box store.

FLASHBACK
Runny Eggs And Milk

"I was a savage for so many years of my life. There was some seed of determination in me that I was not conscious of. I was mostly consciously getting into trouble and drunk."
~ Daniel Day-Lewis

When I was about sixteen, I decided to go out with some of my friends. I said bye to my mom and dad and headed out for some fun. We were all laughing as we went to a friend's house whose parents were gone. When we arrived, the party was already in full swing and booze was flowing freely. I had never been drunk before and I thought one or two Jell-O shots and a little tequila might be fun. So, I imbibed. I really liked the Jell-O shots and, since we had a designated driver, did more than I had planned. Within an hour or so, I was drunk as a skunk. I felt no pain. Life was wonderful and fun. I laughed and told jokes and just really acted like an idiot.

Soon, it was time to go home and reality set in. What if Mom and Dad were still up? What if they sniffed my breath? What if they just knew I was up to something? I asked my friend to stop and get me some coffee because I heard that helped sober you up. It did not. I popped a breath mint. I still reeked. Holy hell! What would I do? We drove around a little while so that us drunks could clear our heads.

I was the third of my friends to get dropped off. I thought I had my shit together, so I strutted clumsily up the driveway and entered my house. I walked slowly and methodically toward the hall, and suddenly I heard my dad. "Did you have fun, Shorty?" He called me Shorty. I am not short.

"Umm hmm," I muttered as I made my way down the hall. I was concentrating on not wobbling back and forth like a ball in a pinball machine. I was not succeeding.

"Are you going right to bed?" my dad asked.

"Umm hmm," I replied smartly.

I shut my bedroom door quickly and got into my pajamas, then jumped into bed. The room was spinning. I put one foot on the floor like one of my friends had told me to do if this happened. It did not help.

I finally drifted off to sleep.

The next morning, at 7:00 a.m., my dear daddy swung open my door with a bang. "Good morning, honey!" he bellowed at the top of his lungs. "How are you feeling?"

"Fine," I whispered, clutching my head. Then I noticed that he had a tray piled high with food.

"Here, honey, I fixed you breakfast in bed because I love you." He was still talking at a decibel that could break a wineglass.

He then plopped on my bed with a thud. My stomach rumbled. I was dying. He put the tray down on my bed with a flourish as I struggled to sit upright. I could not let him know that I was hungover. I had to maintain. And I came close until I looked at the food on the tray. There were about a dozen runny scrambled eggs, close to ten slices of limp, soggy bacon, and a glass of milk that would have filled a two-liter bottle. I. TURNED. GREEN!

My dad was smiling like a damned Cheshire cat while holding up a fork full of the eggs and forcing them into my mouth. "Try these, baby. They look so good even if they are a tad bit runny." He was still screaming.

My head throbbed; my stomach churned. I felt that I was truly going to die as he forced another bite into my mouth. This time when the eggs hit my lips, I gagged a little.

"Here, have some milk to wash that down. I know how you like milk." Pictures were shaking on the wall from his continued yelling.

I tried to take a sip, but the milk propelled me from the bed to the bathroom, where I totally lost my cookies…and the bits of egg and milk.

"I'll leave your breakfast here in your room so that you can finish eating after you get through in the bathroom." God, could that man not speak in a normal tone of voice?

"Umm hmm," I blathered in a very low voice. I vomited again. And again. And one more time.

I was finally able to crawl back to my room. I put the offensive food on my dresser, grabbed two Tylenol out of my purse, and crawled back in bed.

Daddy never mentioned this again, but I had received the message. If getting drunk meant runny eggs and milk…lesson learned. Until the next time.

A Totally True Text Message
You're Doing WHAT???

Bubba: Mom, is the wedding going to start soon?

Me: Yes. The music has started to play. Where are you?

Bubba: I'm pooping.

Me: WHAT?

Bubba: I'm in the bathroom pooping.

Me: This is your sister's wedding and you have to walk the girls down the aisle.

Bubba: I can't help it Mom. My belly hurts.

Me: BUBBA, GET OUT HERE.

Bubba: I'm trying Mom but when ya gotta go ya gotta go.

Me: No, you hold it and get out here like you are supposed to.

Bubba: I'm almost done! I'll be there ASAP.

Me: Too late. Your brother is walking the girls down the aisle. Just run and get into your place.

Bubba: Here I come. I'll make this look good!

Me: You have toilet paper on the bottom of your shoe...EPIC FAIL!

Going For A Walk

> "Every dog has his day, unless he loses his tail, then he has a weak-end."
> ~ June Carter Cash

As I've said, our newly adopted dog, Mr. Bubby, came to us as an abused and abandoned pup. He shivered any time that any human got near him or when the wind blew or when something was different in the house like a chair being pulled out or a towel hanging on a doorknob. He would hide for hours. I decided that I should acclimate him to people, places, and things by taking him for walks. Sweetie said that was a great idea and that she would walk with us. Fun! Family time. Right? Umm...not so much.

Bright and early one Saturday morning we headed out with a harnessed Mr. Bubby. We left the other dogs at home as we felt that it would be better to familiarize him alone. The shakes began immediately as he stepped out the front door and realized he was going to have to actually go outside. Off we went, Sweetie whistling, me tugging at our dog, and Mr. Bubby straining against me...hard. Who knew a dog full of fear could be so strong? I was determined to adapt him to his surroundings, however, so I just kept on pulling him.

Finally, he began to walk slowly. He was still

shaking but he had a look in his eye that I mistook for bravery. Man, was that a mistake. We were about two hundred yards from our house when Mr. Bubby suddenly started to jerk a bit. Sweetie and I were excited. Was he going to get it now and pull me up the sidewalk like I had pulled him? Nope. He turned around and glared at me, then pooped a small turd on my new tennis shoes. Then, with a show of brute force, he ducked out of his harness and ran right to the middle of the street where he proceeded to finish taking a shit and staring me down like he was shooting me a bird.

Sweetie and I ran toward our now free pup, but Mr. Bubby was good. He ran straight to some bushes in a neighbor's yard and began to climb under shrubs and through plants. A lady came out of the house and yelled, "What are you doing in my backyard? Get out now or I'm calling the cops!"

Sweetie hung back to try to calm the lady since I was already ass-deep in the foliage. I could hear her trying to explain. "Ma'am, I'm very sorry that we are in your yard, but our dog got loose and we are trying to get him."

"Yeah, yeah, that's what all burglars say when trying to case the joint," she screeched.

"Burglars? We are your neighbors. We're just trying to get our dog," Sweetie replied calmly.

I was not calm. I was crawling under cutty stuff and through poison ivy. I had bougainvillea stuck in my armpits and pieces of rust from a wheelbarrow stuck in my hair. "Mr. Bubby, come here. It's mommy..." I was pleading as well as bleeding.

"SWEETIE, GET OVER HERE!" I cried. "He's going to dart into another yard and I need you to stop him."

Sweetie came running and squatted with her arms out—much like a rodeo clown—and bounced back and forth. "I've got him if he comes this way."

The neighbor lady screamed, "I'm calling the police right now. Get out of my yard!"

"Oh, shut up," I shrieked. "My armpits are bleeding and there is poison ivy up my ass. This is not how one 'cases the joint.' Are you crazy?"

Mr. Bubby was underneath her outbuilding by this time. Tucked good and tight in the corner. I could not reach him. No one could unless they were about a size two and six foot seven, and I was definitely not. I scooched and ooched and all I was doing was tightening the damn poison ivy, to which I am highly allergic, up around my tweeter. This was not how I expected the day to go.

I grabbed a stick and tried to push it back toward Mr. Bubby. Then I let out a primal yell. It was no stick. It was a snake. I slung that mother as far as I could. Mr. Bubby took this moment to dart from the shed.

Sweetie was on the ball and grabbed him like a calf that had been roped. "I've got him," she bellowed. "Honey, come on out. I've got him."

"I can't get out. I have poison ivy wrapped from my ankle to my tweeter. Help me!" I begged.

"Honey, I can't let go of Mr. Bubby. He'll run off again," she said. "Let me take him home first."

"What the hell? I have to lay under this damned wheelbarrow, tied up with poison ivy and flowers in my armpits? Are you kidding me?" I was really screaming now.

"It won't take me long. I promise."

AND. SHE. LEFT!

After about five minutes, I heard the lady of the house talking to someone and telling them, "She's out there. Under the bougainvillea, Officers. Get her."

I dropped my face into the dirt. I was going to jail for lying in the damn weeds while trying to rescue my dog. Are there even charges against that?

"Ma'am, can you come out of there please? We need to talk to you."

"I can't get out because the ivy is up around my tweeter...help me, please," I begged.

The officers each grabbed a leg and pulled me out slowly as I sniffled.

"What were you doing under there?" Officer Number One asked.

"I was trying to get my dog." I sniffled.

"Where is the dog now?" Officer Number Two questioned.

"Umm...my wife grabbed him and took him home and I couldn't get out from under the weeds..." I blathered.

"So, you weren't trying to rob the place?" This from Officer Number One.

"No, I just wanted to get my dog..." I trailed off.

"Okay, okay, you look honest and I see no evidence of wrongdoing here, so I believe you. Would you like a ride home?" Number Two inquired.

"Let me get this poison ivy out of my tweeter, and then I'd love one." I answered.

We haven't walked Mr. Bubby since!

I Will Grill Him

"After a good dinner one can forgive anybody, even one's own relations."
~ Oscar Wilde

Sweetie and I were out on the patio one evening just enjoying the weather and talking about anything and everything. The subject turned to Thanksgiving when Sweetie asked, "Have you talked with Sissy to see if she's coming over for Thanksgiving dinner?"

"Why, yes, I asked her today and she said that both she and Steven were coming," I replied.

"Oh, I thought that she didn't have him this year for the holidays," she said.

"He whose name shall not cross my lips has to work so he asked if they could switch days. Of course, she said yes, so I guess we do get him." I smiled.

"How about the 'friend/boyfriend person.' Is he coming as well?" Sweetie asked while smiling in an annoying self-satisfied manner.

"Well, umm...err...she, uh, said that she wanted him to come as well since he has no family here." Sweetie does not like strangers in the house. The "friend/boyfriend person" was basically a stranger. This did not please Sweetie. AT. ALL.

Sweetie snarled a bit and said, "Well, if he comes, I hope that he's prepared to answer a lot of questions because I will fucking grill him."

"No, Sweetie, you can't do that. It will make things tense."

"So what? It's about time that he answered several things that I have been wondering about. They've been seeing each other as 'friends' for months now."

"Like what type of questions? What do we have to know just to eat turkey with the guy?" I asked.

"Well, I want to know his intentions. Steven is involved and I want to make sure that he is getting all the attention that he needs," she replied. "Plus, if the 'friend/boyfriend person' plans to be a part of their lives long term, I need to know about his job and what his plans for the future are regarding income."

"This is a holiday. You can't grill hi—"

"This is my house. I can do what I damn well please. I can ask any questions, say anything I think—"

I butted in and said, "No, you can't do that."

"Why? If he comes in my house as a guest, I can say what I want."

"But that's not the time to grill someone and, well, you just can't do it," I said beseechingly.

"Tell me why. Why can't I do it? You are not giving me a reason," she demanded.

"Well…uh…it's…" I stammered as I began to pace around the patio. "It is the Law of Thanksgiving!"

Sweetie barked with laughter. "The what?"

"The, umm, Law of Thanksgiving," I said smartly.

"That is not a thing." Sweetie snorted. "You are just making shit up."

"Oh, no, Sweetie. I am not making it up. It is a real thing. Didn't you follow the Law of Thanksgiving when you were little? It's kinda of like the Law of

Christmas..."

"No, because it is not a law. You just don't want me to grill the 'friend/boyfriend person,' that's all."

"You have to believ—" I started.

"Tell me what the Law of Thanksgiving entails."

"It's sort of like the 'Law of Not Taking Slushies into Wally World.' Remember the time I saved you from possible trouble when I told you about that law. Huh? You remember that, right? These laws are vague and not many people know all about them. They are passed down through the generations. I'm just doing my best to protect you from breaking any of these old obscure laws."

"Yeah, yeah, go on. I can't wait to hear this..."

"Well, first, umm...you have to respect everyone and their beliefs."

"I will do that of course," she acquiesced.

I paced and walked into the house. Sweetie followed. "Come on. You know the law. Tell me."

"Well...err...There is no shouting at each other."

Sweetie nodded her head. "I don't shout."

"Okay. Well, in section three, line eight, it says that there is no grilling allowed."

"This must be a long law if there are sections." Sweetie shook her head.

"Oh, it is quite long, and I can't remember all of it but I do remember those things. Oh, and in section seven, line four, it says that you can't ask any questions pertaining to jobs or money."

By this time, Sweetie was guffawing. "That I can't promise not to ask about."

"No, Sweetie. Now that you know the laws, you must follow them."

"Or what?" she asked.

"Well, the police could get involved and you certainly don't want that."

"You are so making this shit up. How would the police know if I grilled someone in my own home?"

"Well, the 'friend/boyfriend person' could call them if he knows the law," I answered.

"The 'friend/boyfriend person' is too afraid of me to call the cops no matter what I do." She was still snickering. "And he probably does not know the 'laws' anyway."

"Well, what if he does?" I inquired.

"Too bad for him. If he expects to come into my house for an extended period of time, I. WILL. GRILL. HIM. Law be damned." Sweetie let out a whoop of laughter.

I shook my head in despair. This would be a long holiday. I could not make her believe in the Law of Thanksgiving. Just wait until I have to explain the Law of Christmas.

The Sick Day

"I was feeling sick as the proverbial donkey."
~ Mick McCarthy

Sweetie never stays home sick. She is very funny about that. I have seen her walking out the doors holding her ass in her hands just to save a personal day. Imagine my surprise one fine Wednesday when she walked down the stairs, still in her pajamas, to tell me that she was taking a sick day.

"I have to stay home today, hun. I am just so sick that I don't think I can make it to work," she coughed pitifully.

"OH. MY. GOD," I said worriedly. "You never miss work! What's wrong with you? Are you dying? Should we go to the hospital?"

"No, I just have a headache and body aches and a cough," she answered. "I'll be fine with some rest. I'll just stay in bed and you go about your day."

With that, she headed back up to the bedroom. I was standing in the middle of the living room slack-jawed at the fact that she was sick enough not to go to work. What should I do? Soup! Chicken noodle soup is good when you're sick. So, I headed into the kitchen to fix some. I opened the cabinet and went through the many cans of soup. No chicken noodle anywhere. There was, however, some New England clam chowder and clams are kinda like chicken...

right? They both have white meat. I cooked that and rushed it up to Sweetie.

"Here, Sweetie. I made you some soup. Soup is good for you when you are sick. Eat up!" I said proudly.

"What the hell? What kind of soup is that? It reeks. Also, it is six thirty a.m. Who eats soup before the sun comes up?" Hrrrumph. She was being quite belligerent. I was only trying to make her feel better. I am a born caretaker after all.

"Please just let me sleep," she begged.

"Do you want or need anything, Sweetie…"

"NO! I want to go to sleep."

"Sheesh. Okay. You sleep while I go search your symptoms on Dr. Google."

"Ugggh. Whatever." And she closed her eyes.

I ran down to the living room and got my laptop to research Sweetie's symptoms. I plugged in her symptoms and the first thing to pop up was Coxsackievirus. Coxsackievirus is an enterovirus that can also cause flu-like symptoms, rash on hands or feet, or in rare cases, inflammation of the heart (myocarditis) or brain (encephalitis). Coxsackieviruses are RNA viruses that may cause disease of muscles, lungs, and heart. This alarmed me, so I ran up the stairs and peeked under the covers to check for any rashes. None there. Whew, this coxsackievirus sounded scary, so I was glad that Sweetie didn't have that. Back to the computer I went.

Valley fever is a fungal infection that starts in the lungs and causes mild flu-like symptoms. Valley fever is a disease caused by a fungus that gets into your body through your lungs from dirt or soil. It can make you feel like you have a cold or the flu and may cause a rash. Valley fever can be deadly. Hmm. MAY cause a rash. This could be bad. "Sweetie, have you been digging in the dirt lately?" I bellowed so that she could hear me.

"No, I most certainly have not," she croaked. "Please leave me alone. I just need rest."

I continued my search. Tuberculosis! Tuberculosis usually infects the lungs, causing a bad cough with blood, chest pain, fever, chills, and fatigue. "Sweetie," I said in a calm voice so as not to disturb her. "I think you may have tuberculosis. Did you ever have a TB test?"

"For god's sake, woman. I just feel bad! I do not have tuberculosis."

"It could be sarcoidosis," I whispered.

"Dammit, I just have a cold or the flu or something."

FLUIDS! Fluids are good for the flu. I ran to the kitchen to get her some. I loaded a tray with milk, water, orange juice, Sprite, some suspicious-looking cranberry juice, then ran to the bedroom. "Here, Sweetie," I said proudly. "I brought you fluids. Dr. Google says that fluids are good for the cold or flu."

Sweetie just rolled her eyes at me and turned over. "Go away..." She trailed off.

Well, how's that for being grateful? I was just trying to make her well and she won't let me help. I grabbed a washcloth and wet it. Then I snuck up the steps and lay it gently on her forehead just like my momma used to do for me. Did I ever mention that Sweetie is quite jumpy? Well, she is. She screamed and jumped so high that she almost clutched the ceiling with her nails. Maybe I should have made the cloth warm. Oh well, next time.

"GET. OUT," she said in a loud rasp. "Please, I beg of you. Just go do your thing somewhere else. Anywhere else."

I walked down the stairs pouting. It was just 8:00 a.m. and I thought I needed a short nap. This caretaking was a tiring business. My mom was a nurse, and I had no idea how she did it all the time.

After my half-hour nap, I awoke with a start. BEDSORES! I ran up the stairs to turn Sweetie. I didn't want her to get bedsores after all. I slipped my hands gently under her sleeping form and went to flip her to her side. She let out a primal yell that I am sure the neighbors heard. She scampered off the other side of the bed and took a karate stance at me while yelling, "HIYAAA."

"Don't, Sweetie," I yelped. "It's just me."

"For the love of all that's holy, woman, what part of 'leave me alone' don't you understand?"

"I just want to help you," I pouted. "Can I get you anything?"

"Some sleep. That's all, just sleep," she murmured.

As she crawled back in the bed, I tucked in the covers around her. She sniffled and rolled her eyes at the same time. She kind of looked like Uncle Fester but with hair.

I headed back downstairs and vacuumed and dusted and just in general tried to keep busy so that I would leave Sweetie alone, but Dr. Google called my name again. I looked up sarcoidosis once more. I just knew all the symptoms fit. I noticed a symptom that I missed before. Red eyes. I knew Sweetie may get angry, but I could be saving her life. I tippy-toed up the stairs and into our room. I skulked over to the bed and gently raised one of Sweetie's eyelids. I was right. It was RED! Then I felt a smack right to the hand that was holding her eyelid open.

"Owie, why'd you do that?" I asked.

"Well, you stuck your finger in my eye and it startled me so I struck out," she said. "Can't you just please leave me alone? I'm begging you."

"Sure," I said. "I'm sorry, Sweetie. I just wanted to take care of you."

While back downstairs, eating bonbons and watching *The View*, I heard some rustling in the bedroom. "Sweetie," I yelped in fear. "Are you having seizures?"

"No, I am not," she said while coming down the stairs fully dressed. "I am going to work."

"Work? You can't go to work like this, you could spread your sarcoidosis."

"I do not have sarcoidosis! I have the flu or something like that. I am going to work so that I can get some rest," she said, teeth grinding.

And out the door she went.

Hrrrumph, see if I ever take care of Sweetie if she feels ill again. If that's the thanks I get for trying to save her life, she can just take care of herself. At least until she's sick again.

Douche What???

"Laughter and tears are both responses to frustration and exhaustion. I myself prefer to laugh, since there is less cleaning up to do afterward."
~ Kurt Vonnegut

Sweetie and I got very ill a while back. We both had some sort of uber respiratory infection. Now, let it be known that Sweetie is a germaphobe, so she announced, as we were lying in the bed hacking up our lungs, that we must *douche* the house! I was sick and I thought my fever must have spiked when I heard her say "douche the house." Surely, I was hearing things. She must be talking out of her head. Maybe it was her temperature that had spiked and she was simply delusional.

I shook her and said, "Sweetie, you can't douche a house. A douche is for your tweeter. Are you Okay? The fever has made you a bit out of your head. Just go back to sleep."

"No, I am not out of my head. If we want to get better, we must douche the house," she replied.

"How does one douche a house?" I asked.

"Come on and I'll show you how." And she crept out of the bed and began to crawl toward the stairs.

I went to the bathroom in order to grab my supplies. I had to do some digging, but I finally found what I needed. I slogged down the stairs carrying a

Summer's Day douche so I could help Sweetie. "Here, I found a douche, now tell me what to do with it that will help us get better."

"What in the world are you doing with that?" Sweetie asked.

"It's a douche for us to douche the house. Isn't that what you wanted?" I had never douched a house before so, obviously, I didn't know that one did not need an actual douche in order to douche a house. It sounded good to me.

"No. That is not how you do it. Come on, let me show you." Sweetie proceeded to show me how one douches a house.

FYI, it is a hell of a lot of work. I figured this out as I was lying on my back cleaning the undersides of the cabinets. Really? Who does that?

Sweetie then said, "I am going to run to the Handy Depot to rent a steam cleaner. Why don't you go get the carpet knife and cut up the carpet in the basement while I am gone?"

"Excuse me?" I said with my mouth agape. "You want me to cut up the carpet? Seriously?"

"Well, yes. How else can we get rid of the germs that are trapped in there? It must come up," she demanded.

"Umm...where is the carpet knife?" I asked, hoping that it was lost in her workshop.

"I'll get it for you," she offered kindly...NOT!

Sweetie came up the stairs from her workshop and slapped the knife in my hand like a nurse would do a doctor in surgery. "Knife! Here you go. Now get busy." And she headed out the door, eyes gleaming red.

I immediately plopped down on the couch and

fell over. I was too sick to cut up the carpet. Then I remembered her red eyes and decided that cutting the carpet in the basement would be a better idea than facing the wrath of Sweetie. Down the basement stairs I went. I began to cut up the carpet that was barely a year old. I rolled each piece up and dragged the sections outside by the trash can.

Sweetie arrived back from Handy Depot. She then looked downstairs to see how far along I was on cutting up the carpet. I was snoring on a section that was half cut. I was sick after all.

"Babe, get up." She was wielding the steam cleaner over her head. "This will get rid of those nasty microorganisms. We must finish the douching of the house. We can't afford to get sick all the time, so the germs must go!" She put a mask over her mouth and nose.

"Sweetie, I am sick. You are sick. Let's go back to bed and we can do this later. I swear the carpet will not kill us today."

"You just don't get it," she mumbled through the mask. "You go to bed and I will finish douching the house. But first please take this antibacterial spray and spray everything in the house. Wipe down anything that is made of wood."

I grabbed the spray and began to spray everything from the floor to the walls to the furniture and even the dogs. I got to the guest bed, fell over, and went fast asleep. When Sweetie came to find me, everything around me smelled like Clorox. The house was gleaming. But WE WERE. STILL. SICK! Fat lotta good it did to douche the house. I grabbed my Summer's Day and opened the top and proceeded to squeeze out every drop on our polished floors, then washed down walls.

"There, now the whole house is douched for real. Can we go to bed now? Please?" I pled. Sweetie just put another mask on and started to wipe the douche water off the floor and walls. "Good idea, babe. This fights bacteria. Do we have any more?"

Sigh

Drive-by Farting

"If I could light my own farts I could fly to the moon or at least Uranus."
~ Robin Williams

One lovely Saturday morning, Wally World called out to Sweetie and me. Well, it called out to me, as Sweetie hates the store with a blinding passion, but it was calling anyway. There were many things that we needed around the house, and everyone knows that Wally World is the less expensive alternative. Everyone but Sweetie, that is.

"Come on, Sweetie, it's time to make our way to the happiest place on earth."

"We are going to Disney? I'll go there with you any ole day if we can just skip Wally World. I'll drive...I'll buy the ticke—" she started.

"No, not Disney. Quit stalling, and let's go and get this thing done," I said.

"OH. MY. GOD. Please don't make me go." Her eyes were fluttering and she looked a bit faint, so I grabbed her hand and dragged her toward the truck.

"Please, please don't make me do this. I will pay extra at any store. Please."

"Oh, suck it up, buttercup. It will be fine."

Sweetie crawled dejectedly into the driver's seat and off we went for some fun.

Upon arriving at Wally World, Sweetie started

whining again. "Please don't make me go in there…"

"Ahhh, come on. What's the worst that could happen? Someone will cough on you while walking by? Sheesh, you are so delicate."

"I am delicate! And nasty germs could be passed in the coughing scenario, so thanks for putting that into my head," she grumbled.

We entered the store and grabbed a cart. Sweetie immediately took over half of the provided antibacterial wipes and proceeded to wipe the entire buggy from top to bottom and end to end. You could have eaten off of the damn thing.

We made our way through the brightly lit store, me joking and Sweeting dragging behind like Quasimodo. After picking up necessities like toothpaste and dental floss, we stopped to look at hairspray on the endcap of the aisle. While standing there arguing over the best type to get, me going for the cheapest and Sweetie voting for the more expensive but most advertised brand, a rancid smell washed over us both. Our eyes began to water. Sweetie looked around and saw a stock associate bent doubled over in order to put things on the bottom shelf.

"He farted," Sweetie stage-whispered. "Good Lord, I think something crawled up in him and died."

We grabbed the most expensive hairspray and ran from the rank aisle.

"Sheesh, that was awful. I have NEVER smelled a fart that bad," Sweetie said.

"Sure, you have," I answered. "Remember the time that you ate the bad shrimp at—"

"Zip it," Sweetie said while making a cross-lip movement with her fingers.

"Wow, you are still sensitive about that, huh?

It's okay, Sweetie. Gas happens to the best of us."

"Stop," she pleaded.

We went forward on our quest for a new shower curtain liner. As we looked and argued about the best type to buy, another wave of stench washed over us.

"Dear Lord. Did that stock boy follow us?" Sweetie asked, looking around.

"No," I said. "But a pregnant woman is one aisle over and you know that pregnant women always have gas: silent but violent!"

"What the hell is wrong with these people? Can't they just go to the restroom to fart like normal people do?" Sweetie asked while holding her nose.

"Hmm, I guess they just don't have the home training that we do, hun," I said with a wan smile.

We grabbed a clear shower curtain liner and ran from the spot. "Let's just go to the grocery department and see if our luck is better on that side of the store."

I answered with a nod.

We walked at a fast clip to the soda aisle—I drink a lot of diet soda, so this was a staple. We loaded up the cart with no reeking smells around us. Sweetie gave me the thumbs-up and we sauntered over to the laundry detergent aisle. Sweetie was reaching high for our brand. Yes, we have a brand...Sweetie is very particular.

As she reached higher, a barely audible *pfffttt* was heard. There were quite a few people on this aisle, and within seconds a foul-smelling stench hit us all in the face. Sweetie looked around and shook her head back and forth as if to say, "It wasn't me." People scrunched their faces and stared.

We threw the detergent into the cart and ran for the cheese.

"What the fuck?" Sweetie squealed. "Are people just so rude that they fart anywhere?"

A shopper from the clothes detergent aisle walked by and shook her head at Sweetie.

"You know that the people in the detergent aisle think it was you since you were stretching, right?" I asked.

Sweetie's face turned a bright red. "No way," she screeched. "I am innocent in all this. Let's get out of here. NOW! People are looking at me oddly."

"So what? Let them look. We have shopping to do, woman."

"I'm done. You asked what was the worst that could happen, and this is it. Forget the coughing on me scenario, farting rancidly in public is the very worst. Especially when people think it is me." She grabbed the cart and headed toward the cashiers with a purpose.

We were knocking against people as we hurried toward the front of the store. "Slow down, Sweetie," I begged. I was having a hard time keeping up.

Another shopper looked at Sweetie and shook his head in disdain. She walked faster. "Dammit! Stop staring," she yelped.

I started giggling. This was shaping up to be a great day.

"STOP. IT! This is not funny. Everyone thinks it was me and I am innocent," she said with agitation.

We reached the checkout and did our business when I spotted a shop specializing in sub sandwiches. It was right in the store. "Oh, Sweetie, can we have a sub?" I asked.

"Might as well. What's the worst it can do now? Make us gaseous?" she said with a snarky tone.

We walked over to the shop and she went in to get us lunch while I waited by the door. A disgusting odor wafted over, leaving a green fog. Sweetie walked right through it. "What the hell?" she said at the top of her lungs, snot running from her nose as if she had been stink-bombed. "Can you people just fart somewhere else?" Then she headed, in a huff, out the door.

I followed with a knowing grin. One cannot help when gas hits, and farts happen. I should know. It had just happened to me. I'd never tell her that, though. A lady has her secrets, you know.

It Comes With The Territory

"Some women can't say the word lesbian...even when their mouth is full of one."
~ Kate Clinton

Early one Saturday, Sweetie and I were working in the front yard—her idea, not mine! I hate working in the heat. My hair gets all curly and stuff. We were planting night-blooming jasmine and digging up weeds. I know. Fun, right? We had been at this, with me bitching, for about an hour and a half. I was *thrilled* to say the least. Sweat was pouring down my butt crack and my face...but the butt crack was worse...far worse. Ick! All of a sudden, up popped our neighbor John. He looked bewildered. He was waving his arms animatedly, so Sweetie and I stopped what we were doing and walked over to him.

"I just saw a dog running around the other neighbor's yard, back and forth to the fence. It looked scared and like it was confused," he said breathily.

"Aww, poor thing," I replied. "What do you want us to do about it?" I was testy from all of the butt crack sweat and really didn't care about his problems.

"How can we help?" Sweetie asked. She liked yard work. I did not. As a matter of fact, it sucks. "Why not just go knock on the door and tell them?"

"Well, I don't know them, and I think they are gone anyway. I think the poor dog got out of the side gate and now it is scared," his reply came.

"And…" I said as I pulled my shorts out of my moist butt crack. I was not in the mood.

"Well, you see, they are umm, well, like you ladies, and I thought the dog might just come to one of you gals…"

"You mean that they are women?" I asked. I was being a smart-ass and I knew it. I did not care. I was tired and had perspiration EVERYWHERE.

"Well, uh, no they are *like you*," he said with a drop of his wrist. "Don't you know them?"

"What do you mean that they are 'like us,'" Sweetie asked, dropping her wrist as well. She was the sarcastic one now. "You must mean that they are female. Right?"

"Umm, no. They are LIKE YOU. Ya know?" He dropped his hand at the wrist exaggeratedly. I thought it might break right off. How interesting that would be.

"Oh, they work in the yard?" I asked.

"No. Uh, one of them is short and the other is tall, and one has brown hair and the other is a blonde," he answered uncomfortably. "Just like you two."

"Nope, don't know them," Sweetie answered with a red face.

"So, like, their house is like yours and they have a fence," John continued. He was digging himself deeper and deeper in a hole.

"Most houses in this neighborhood are *sort* of like ours and pretty much all of them have fences as well," I replied, not letting him off the hook.

"It's the house right next to me," he practically screamed. "They are always together and they, errr, look like you ladies and they wear cargo shorts and have a truck and..."

"Ohhhh...You mean that they are lesbians," Sweetie said. "Why didn't you say so in the first place?"

John looked a wee bit scared like maybe Sweetie would pop him in the nose.

"Honey, go inside and get the *General Book of Lesbians* and look the neighbors' phone number up. I'm sure they would not want their sweet dog running loose."

"A book? There's a book?" John looked perplexed.

"Why of course," I said while running into the house. "How else can we girls find each other?"

Momentarily, I ran back out and screamed, "I have the number. We can call them now."

John looked puzzled. "There *is* a book," he whispered as if it were magic. "Wow!"

"Don't you heterosexuals have a *book*?" I asked. "How inconvenient for you."

John looked perplexed again.

"NO, dumbass," Sweetie answered. "We don't have a *book*. We don't even know the neighbors or their phone numbers. Go catch the damn dog and put it back in the fence. Everything will be right in the world. And, by the way, the limp wrist is not the universal symbol for lesbians." She made a V with her first two fingers and put her tongue through and wiggled it. "This is!"

John took off running like a scalded dog toward his house. He was moving at a really fast clip for a middle-aged man. I heard the door slam.

"Let's go get their dog now. We'd hate it if ours went missing," I said as I high-fived Sweetie. And we did. The poor thing must have recognized the lesbian in us as he ran straight to us as we walked down the road. Crisis averted by the lesbians.

Humdinger

"Shopping is better than sex. If you're not satisfied after shopping you can make an exchange for something you really like."
~ Adrienne Gusoff

Sweetie and I rarely fight. But one Saturday, we had a humdinger. Sweetie had opened my closet door to get a sweater and a shitload of boxes had fallen out on her. I had been shopping on Home Shopping Network once more. She let out a primal yell, "WHAT HAVE YOU BEEN BUYING...YET AGAIN?" You see, I am bipolar and shopping is what I do in a manic state. And when I am in a manic state, I buy. I buy a lot!

"Well, I needed a new camera and a new outfit and some shoes to match and new shoes need purses to match..."

"STOP," she yelped. "You don't 'need' anything. You have clothes folded in baskets that you have never even worn. Why would you need more? You also have a hundred purses and three hundred pairs of shoes... in every color."

"Well, that is a bit of an exaggeration, don't you think? I have twenty purses and fifty pairs of shoes and not one shoe is red unless you count the dark pink as reddish..."

"Stop it! You can't just shop all willy-nilly. You

could use that money for other stuff."

I had to giggle here. Willy-nilly is a funny word don't you think?

"Stop giggling. This is not funny. I am going to throw all of this shit, except the camera, in the pool. That way maybe you will learn," Sweetie blurted loudly.

"In the pool? Oh, no you don't. Those are mine and I want them and need them and…"

"You NEED an outfit that is two sizes too small?" she asked.

"Well, I am on a diet, and you don't want me to go around naked when the weight just drops off of me, do you?" I inquired smartly.

"You can buy new clothes when you need them. Not months before." She was starting to yell now. Hrrrumph!

"I can yell too, you know." But I couldn't think of anything to yell about, so I just stood in the corner of the room and pouted. I am really, really good at pouting. It's a great skill of mine.

Sweetie scooped up the boxes that contained clothing, shoes, and a purse and headed outside to the pool. She stood there with her arms raised as if to drop them into the depths. This set me into motion. Outside I ran.

"Sweetie, you can't just throw those in the pool. It will ruin them," I said at the top of my voice.

"Well, you should have thought of that before you bought them," she shouted.

The neighbors went quiet as I began to run after her. Round and round the pool we went, her hollering about spending too much money and me pleading for her not to throw my stuff away. We got tired after about the third lap and stopped to catch our breath. Then, for some reason, I began to giggle and cry at the same time. She was definitely NOT laughing or crying. She was steaming. But this was funny…sort of…if I got to keep my stuff.

I threatened, loudly, between guffaws and snorts, "I will call the police if you throw my things in the pool and ruin them. They are mine and I paid for them."

"Well, I will have you locked up in the loony bin for shopping rehab. There is such a thing you know. It's like the 'Shopping Act' or something."

"Psssh, there is no such thing. Besides, who would take care of the dogs and the housework while I was lounging in the nuthouse?" (I know about all the lounging that is done in the nuthouse as I have been there before, but that's a story for another day.)

Suddenly, a bright blue shirt hit the water. I shrieked, "STOP. THAT. NOW!"

"Nope. It's all going in the pool." She was a woman on a mission now. She pulled back her arms in order to toss everything.

This spurred me into action. I took off running, taking her by surprise. I grabbed the clothing and wrestled it from her. It dropped into the grass but at least it was safe now. Sweetie reached to try and pick it up again, but her foot slipped on the pool deck and she fell toward the pool. I grabbed for her and—you guessed it—we both went ass-over-teakettle into the water. Did I mention it was January and cold outside? Well, I mean it was cold for South Florida, which was about sixty-five degrees. Don't judge. We are not used to such arctic temperatures. Both of us swam to the shallow end of the pool to get out. We were shivering.

Sweetie was fuming and I was chuckling. This had been a great adventure. For me, anyway.

"I mean it. I will commit you to 'Shopping Rehab' if you do that again," she said tartly. Think of the money that you spent on nothing."

"NOTHING?" I screeched. "I love and need those things."

"Give me your credit cards. Now! I mean it," she whispered through chattering teeth.

"Why? Do you want to go shopping too? Can I go with you? I'll need to get dried off and put on fresh makeup," I said smartly.

"Aaargh!" she shouted with her hands clenched in her dripping hair.

I guess shopping was out of the question for now. Just wait until she finds out that I have a QVC card.

FLASHBACK
What's Wrong With Her

"In the pregnancy process I have come to realize how much of a burden is on the female partner. She's got a construction zone going on in her belly."
~ Al Roker

My oldest son was just five months old when I found out that I was pregnant again. Yep, I'm that smart. When I got the news, I just sat down and cried. Another baby...so soon. What was I thinking? I wasn't thinking...I rarely do. I just never took up thinking as a habit. It's really overrated. But I guess sometimes, like this one, it would have been a great idea.

My pregnancy went wonderfully if you consider wonderful to include ankles the size of elephant legs, boobs the size of watermelons, a bladder the size of an almond, and puking like a fountain. See, just peachy! The months dragged—I mean flew—by blissfully. It was a girl this time, and I had always wanted a girl.

When the time came to deliver the sweet child, my parents were there for support. I woke up in labor and let my mom know. She, in turn, let my dad know that we all needed to get ready to go to the hospital. When everyone was dressed, we headed to the car. My dad said that he would drive alone because if I started having the baby in the car, he'd be damned if he would be there to help with the grossness that childbirth could be. Anyway, off we went, dad in his own car and the rest of us in mine.

My ex was speeding because this baby seemed to be coming faster than the first, and he hit some railroad tracks on a hill that sent us flying and started me cussing. "What the hell did you do that for? You could have knocked the baby out, dammit." Keep in mind that I was in pain.

"I'm sorry. I'll slow down," the ex said.

"For fuck's sake, speed up a bit. At this damn rate the kid will be in college before we get there."

"Umm, Okay."

"Why don't you just let me drive? I can get us there better than you can," I said testily.

"Now, now, calm down. We'll be there in time," reassured my mother.

"Whatever," I murmured.

We arrived at the hospital, and they took me straight back as I seemed to be in the end stages of labor. Hrrrumph. I knew the ex drove too slowly. Why would no one listen to me?

"Where is my daddy? I need my daddy," I yelped.

"He's not here yet," Momma said. "I'm sure he'll be here soon."

"AAAAAAARGH," I yelled. "She's coming now! I feel her head."

"But there's no doctor or nurse in here right now." My ex was panicked.

"Tee-hee...just joking." I get weird when I'm in pain.

My momma chimed in. "That was not nice."

"AAAAAAAARGH," I screamed again.

"Not funny," retorted the ex.

"Not joking," I said. "She really is coming now.

Get someone. NOW!"

The doctor and nurses came in and checked me again and said it was time. They threw my mom out. There was still no sign of my daddy. Then we went about the business of baby birthing.

During the throes of hard labor, I grabbed the ex's hand and twisted it and pulled him down to my face and said, "YOU. DID. THIS. I will kill you."

The ex grew pale. I guess I did seem like a murderer at this point.

Finally, I was pushing. It only took three pushes and my sweet dream of a baby girl came into the world. And there was something wrong, very wrong, with her. She looked like a bird. She had a shock of long black hair and skin the color of a pumpkin. She was skinny and had claws for fingers.

The nurse wrapped her up and pronounced her "perfect." HUH? There was something wrong and they were just trying to spare me the pain.

"Just tell me what is wrong with her," I cried. "I can take it."

"She's just a bit jaundiced but otherwise healthy," the nurse replied.

"Look at her. She looks like a bird...a bright yellow bird. Don't you lie to me," I said.

My momma had come into the room by that time and was oohing and cooing over my poor yellow bird. "She's just beautiful."

"Momma, don't lie to me. Make them tell me what is wrong with her," I begged.

"Honey, nothing is wrong with her. She is yellow due to jaundice and she is not filled out yet, so she's long and skinny and all that black hair is surprising. But she is healthy."

"Give me drugs," I implored.

"The drugs are before the birth. Not after," answered the nurse.

"I said GIVE. ME. DRUGS!" So, she did. Probably to shut me up.

When I woke, there was a cold hand between my legs and a nurse straddling me and rubbing my belly like you would knead bread dough.

"What the hell are you doing?" I demanded, giving her a karate chop to the shoulder.

"I am massaging your fundus," she replied while rubbing her hurt shoulder.

"FUNGUS? I have a fungus? Is that what is wrong with my baby? I gave her a fungus?"

"No. Your FUNDUS. We massage it so that it stimulates the uterus to contract and helps in slowing any bleeding after childbirth."

"Ohhhhh. Gross. Are you sure it's not a fungus?" I asked

"No, it is a fundus. With a D."

"Whose hand is between my legs? It's freezing."

"That is just a frozen glove to ease the pain."

"Good, because nothing is going between my legs again for a very long time."

The nurse rolled her eyes. "I've heard that before."

"What's wrong with my baby? She is all yellow and skinny and hairy and she looks like a bird."

"Your baby is fine. She is just a little on the, umm, plain side," she replied.

"Hey, don't call my baby plain," I said. "Can you bring her to me?"

"Sure. That way you'll see for yourself that she is fine," she said.

My baby was brought in all swaddled up, and

with a hat and blanket on she looked pretty much okay. The ex came in, too, and was so proud of the little girl that he was about to burst.

"Isn't she beautiful?" he asked.

"Oh, yes," I replied a wee bit sarcastically.

"She's perfect," he boasted proudly.

"Umm hmm. Where's my daddy?" I knew that he'd be honest with me. Everyone was trying to protect me from the truth, but my daddy was honest.

"Let me see if I can find him for you." And he walked away, carrying the baby back to the nursery.

Eventually my dad came sauntering into the all-white room and I asked, "Where have you been? What took you so long to get here?"

"I went the wrong way and got lost," he said with embarrassment.

"LOST? You have lived here most of your life. How in the hell did you get lost?" I asked.

"I was, umm, nervous," he replied.

"Have you seen the baby yet?" I asked.

"Errrrr, yes. Yes, I have," he replied

"And...?"

"And...good job pushing her out."

"Daddy, does she look okay to you, or does she look like a yellow bird?"

"Well, honey, let's just look at it this way. If Big Bird ever dies, she will have a great job!"

See? I knew my daddy would be honest.

Addendum ~ My sweet girl, Sissy, filled out, the jaundice cleared up, and she is now a beautiful young woman. See, honey? I told you this story wasn't all bad. I love you! Does that get me back in your good graces?

Honey, It's February

"If love is the answer, could you rephrase the question?"
~ Lily Tomlin

Sweetie woke me up one early February morning with a hoot. "Honey, it's February. How exciting is that?"

I was still sleeping, so I glanced her way through half-closed eyes and muttered, "Just peachy. Now go back to sleep. It's four o'clock in the morning, for heaven's sake." I was grumpy. Four in the morning. Good grief! So, I drifted back to sleep.

Sweetie shook me...HARD! "But honey, it is February. We must make plans."

I opened one eye. "What the hell? We don't need plans right now." I wasn't seeing her point...if she had one.

I could feel Sweetie pouting. FEEL. IT. I. SAY! I opened my eyes and said, "So, yeah, it's February. Next it will be March. Then April—"

"But February is special," she interrupted. "Think about it. What happens in February? C'mon, you know, don't you?" She had a Cheshire cat grin on her face. It was scary. Have you ever seen your wife looking like a Cheshire cat? Well, consider yourself lucky.

"Why is February special?" I asked. My brain was foggy, and I could think of nothing that was special enough to wake me at the butt crack of dawn.

"Think, honey, think. It happens every year and I am always excited just as you should be." She was rising in enthusiasm now. I was simply baffled.

Suddenly I realized February was the month that Valentine's Day occurred. How sweet. She remembered, and not only that...she was excited about it!

"Aww, Sweetie, it was so sweet of you to remember. Now, can we talk about it when I am fully awake?"

"NO! We must talk about it now. I have phone calls and plans to make. This is so important." She was practically shouting.

"But we have time to make those plans and calls. No one will be awake to take your calls now anyway. It is very sweet of you to be so excited, though," I said.

"But—"

"No buts. Valentine's Day is fourteen days away. You have time to think about gifts and flowers and such. Now, go back to sleep and think about this in the morning."

"Valentine's Day? Is that in February?" she asked.

"Well, yeah. What the heck were you so excited about if not the day of love?" I replied.

"Well, uh...I was uh...thinking of uh... Well, of course I was thinking of Valentine's Day. How smart of you to know that," she stammered.

"I call bullshit," I said with fervor. "What happens in February besides Valentine's Day and a few family birthdays?"

"Well, umm, I was, errr, thinking of a more pressing matter," she said.

"More pressing than giving your true love a

beautiful gift? What could be more pressing than that?" I asked.

"Well, you see, February is the month that we have the septic tank pumped. That is important don't you think?"

"More important than Valentine's Day? Pumping the septic tank...Valentine's Day. Pumping the septic tank...Valentine's Day. Nope, I choose Valentine's Day every single time," I replied testily. I was fully awake by now. And, angry to boot.

"Umm, I was just joking. HA HA. I made a funny, didn't I?"

"No, you were so very serious. How could you put septic pump pumping before Valentine's Day?" I asked. "What were you thinking?"

"Well, uh, you have to poop, and if the septic tank gets full the toilet will back up and flow out on the floor and, uh, well that would be gross...and..." Sweetie was stammering and trying to save face at this point but I wasn't letting her off the hook that easily. So, I faked some tears.

"You would put poop before my lovely Valentine's gift? I can't believe that. I am so very hurt."

"Don't cry," she replied. "Septic tank pumping was just on my mind. I would have remembered Valentine's Day. Really, I would have."

"Yeah, yeah. You just keep telling yourself that. I will forever remember that the septic tank would come before me," I said as a plan formed in my head. "You love the pump more than me. I get it."

"No, I love you more than anything in the world, baby. I would do anything for you. You must know that. Whatever you need or want, just tell me," she said.

"Oh, no, honey. You just get your septic tank pumped. I'll be fine," I replied with a fake catch in my throat. I closed my eyes to go back to sleep. Boy, would I get a great Valentine's Day gift this year. I smiled as I drifted off.

Sweetie, You Got Some 'Splainin' To Do!

"A bargain is something you can't use at a price you can't resist."
~ Franklin P. Jones

As I was polishing the silverware (that's a housewifely duty, right?) one afternoon, Sweetie called to let me know that she was on her way home but would be making a quick stop to do some shopping. Huh? Sweetie was going to go shopping... by herself...with no cajoling from me? The apocalypse was nigh. I could feel it beginning.

"Umm, erm, you're going to do what?" I asked with a croak.

"I'm going shopping," she replied with a chirp.

"Uh, why? Where? What for?" I blathered.

"Just got something I need to go look at," she said cheerfully.

Something was wrong. Sweetie was going shopping, alone, without being prompted and she was happy about it. Oh Lordy. Was it our anniversary? My birthday? Valentine's Day? No, nope, and nada. What the hell was going on? Oooh, she was going to the home shopping store to get nails or a hammer or some tape. Now, THAT made sense.

"Okay, hun. You enjoy yourself and I'll see you

in a bit," I said with relief. I was glad not to have to go to the home shopping store. Now I could paint my nails or walk the dog or anything that didn't have to do with home repair.

Well, I walked the dog, did my nails, changed the sheets, dusted, sang a rousing chorus of "99 Bottles of Beer on the Wall," and Sweetie still wasn't home. I tried calling her but got no answer. I began to get worried. I put dinner in the oven…and took it out when it was done forty-five minutes later. Still no Sweetie. I was beginning to really worry. Should I call the police or a detective or missing person? Sweetie was never late.

"Do they still put missing people's faces on milk cartons?" I wondered.

I was just picking up the phone to call in reinforcements when I heard a rumble in the driveway. I peeked out hoping it was Sweetie. It was not, I saw with dread. It was a big black SUV and she drives a black truck. Oh, geez Louise. Was that the FBI? Was Sweetie in some kind of trouble? Was she on the run? Had she been using code when she called me and was I just too dense to catch on? What the hell was going on? Was Sweetie a drug lord wanted by the cartel and would we have to go into witness protection? What would I tell my kids? Wait, could I even tell my kids if we were being relocated by the feds?

Just at that moment, Sweetie leaped happily out of the driver's side with a gleam in her eye. Huh? Had Sweetie *joined* the FBI? Was this her undercover vehicle?

I ran out the door and fell at Sweetie's feet, hugging them tightly. "You are home. I was so afraid. Why did it take so long? You are never late. I thought we were going to have to be placed in witness protection. When did you join the FBI?" I finally came up for a quick breath.

Sweetie pulled me to a standing position, looked me straight in the eyes, and asked, "What the hell are you jabbering about?"

"You are late. You are never late. I was going to go buy some milk so that I could search all the cartons for your missing person's picture. But you are here now and you are not missing and you are driving a fed's car so I figured you must have joined the FBI or CIA or be working for the cartel…you're not, umm, working for the cartel, are you?"

Sweetie looked at me with eyes that clearly said that she thought that I had lost it. I was very used to that look. She said in a very calm tone, "I told you that I was going shopping. Well, I did, and this is my new car. Isn't she a beauty?"

"You bought a car? That's what you went shopping for? Not a nail gun or a new ceiling fan. A CAR. A whole car!" I screeched.

"Well, buying half a car wouldn't have made any sense, now would it? She's beautiful huh?" she asked, waving her hands like Vanna White.

"A CAR. You were shopping for a car and did not think to mention it to me? I don't even buy peanut butter cups without consulting you and this is…a car. A big ole black SUV with four wheels and everything. And you just bought it." Each word getting louder.

Sweetie clamped her hand over my mouth. "Shush! The neighbors will hear you for gosh sake."

"But…but…but…it's a car. A big ole black SUV. And you bought it. What was wrong with your truck? It was only two years old." I was stammering.

"Get in. Take a look. It's really beautiful and you will love it. Let's take it for a spin!" She was so happy that I couldn't say no. So, I jumped in the passenger seat. There was no way that I was going to drive that vehicle. Nuh-uh. If I wrecked it or scratched or even got footprints inside it, she would likely kill me.

She put it in reverse and off we went. She was grinning from ear to ear, singing along with the radio and speeding a teeny bit to show off. Suddenly, the brakes engaged. Hard! The car said, "Imminent Accident Alert!" And, a warning flashed on the console that said, "PUT BOTH HANDS ON WHEEL!"

We both screamed. What the hell? Did we break the car? Nope, strike that. Did *Sweetie* break the car? I had nothing to do with it. I was only a passenger. No way was this getting blamed on me. I was an *innocent* passenger. I couldn't help it if Sweetie's new car was straight out of *Christine*. That's it, this was all Stephen King's fault. Sweetie put both hands on the steering wheel and slowed to a crawl. We were both frightened. That's when a notification flashed on the console, "Pull over. Driver seems tired. Stop and have a cup of coffee."

That was it. "TAKE ME HOME NOW, SWEETIE. This car is the devil and I want OUT!"

I glanced at Sweetie. She was pasty white. She glanced in my direction and tried to grin looking like Pennywise instead. "Umm, I think we'll just mosey on home now. I really need to read the manual for this thing."

"Ya think?" I replied smarmily. I was still shaking.

We headed back to the house and I jumped out, kneeled, and literally kissed the ground. "Next time you want to go shopping by yourself, just go get a new home-fixing thingy. Those don't try to kill you."

"Are you sure about that?" replied Sweetie in a voice that rivaled Dracula. "A ceiling fan could do quite some damage."

I took off running into the house thinking of things that ceiling fans could do to me. Visions of decapitation floated in through my head. I mostly hate shopping (unless it's lovely manic shopping on QVC!) and even worse, I hate Sweetie shopping…alone!

A Totally True Text Message
A Comedy of Errors

Kris (our close friend who was babysitting our dogs while we were on vacation): How the hell do you get these dogs inside in the morning? I have to go to work and they have already pooped and peed and everything.

Sweetie: LOL. You just stand at the door and say "Come in."

Kris: I did that and they looked at me like I was a moron.

Sweetie: Is it just Mr. Bubby?

Kris: NO! It is all three of them.

Sweetie: Well, you are doing something wrong. They are good doggies. Ask if they want a cookie.

Kris: I am not doing anything wrong. I called them and tried giving them a cookie and then I chased them around the pool four times until I fell and busted my ass. I had hoped to catch them and carry them in. I am now tired as hell and sweaty and have a sore ass. I will need another shower. I don't know what to do now.

Sweetie: I never have a problem. Try again.

Kris (after about ten minutes): Dammit, I tried again and Juno just went to the edge of the fence and laughed at me.

Sweetie: Dogs don't laugh.

Kris: Juno did. I am going to cry.

Sweetie: Oh, buck up and go call them sternly.

They will come.

Kris: No, they won't. They hate me. I'm going to take another shower. I stink.

Sweetie: Oh, for heaven's sake. Take your shower and then try again.

Kris (after fifteen minutes): I came downstairs and the freaking dogs were just sitting down on the rug looking like nothing ever happened.

Sweetie: See, I told you that they were good dogs.

Kris: Whatever.

Sweetie: OK, don't forget to close the curtains and lock up before you leave.

Kris: I won't.

Kris (After about ten minutes): Dammit all, I tried closing the curtains and one fell off and the pole hit me right on my head. I fixed that one and then the other end came down. I put all of your curtains back on the pole and ice on my head then went to lock the back slider and the lock won't go into place. How do I lock this stupid door?

Sweetie: You simply push the lock up.

Kris: I. AM. It is not working.

Sweetie: Make sure it is all the way shut and try again.

Kris: Well that worked. Did I mention that I hate your house?

Sweetie: HA HA!

Kris: Shut up. I am going to work now and I am going to be late and I will blame it all on you.

Kris (After about five minutes): SOMEONE. BROKE. INTO. MY. CAR!

Sweetie turned around laughing, looked at me and said, "Hmm, I guess we are going to need a new dog sitter."

Newfangled Gadgets

"I used to say that whenever people heard my Southern accent, they always wanted to deduct 100 IQ points."
~ Jeff Foxworthy

Santa brought us a newfangled gadget for Christmas. It is called "Alexa" and she does a lot of things around the house like turn on the lights, answer pressing questions like "How old is Susan Sarandon?" (Come on…that is important if you want to compare your facial wrinkles with hers to see who looks the oldest), and make grocery lists. All you have to do is say "Alexa, add pickles to the shopping list" and voila! It is on the list on your cell phone. Cool huh? Well, it is if you don't have a Southern accent… which I do!

I am from North Carolina…way up in the mountains of western North Carolina. I am as Southern as they come. I bless everyone's heart and drawl the word "hun" with the best of them. Some of my friends…Liz McMullen…can't understand half of what I say and only guess at the other half. Evidently, so does Alexa. I found this out when we went grocery shopping one weekend.

While walking up and down the aisles grabbing carrots, tomatoes, and mushrooms that were on our list, we marked them off and they magically disappeared from the file. How cool is that?

Sweetie suddenly stopped mid-aisle and said, "What is 'Climbing young'?"

"Huh?" I said. "Climbing young? I have no idea. Where did you see that? It can't be on the list."

"It's right by the chicken," Sweetie replied.

"Oh, for heaven's sake. That's supposed to be filet mignon. Alexa got it wrong," I snapped.

"Oh, blame it on Alexa, dear," she replied snidely.

We continued our trip through the store, and again Sweetie asked a burning question, "What the hell is 'Smoke Chicka Chicka Saw'?"

"I do not know. I did not say anything like that for certain."

Sweetie began to giggle. I was not amused.

"It's still in the meat section, so does it ring a bell?"

"Oh, for fuck's sake. It is smoked chicken sausage and I said it just like that. SMOKED. CHICKEN. SAUSAGE. Alexa needs a hearing aid," I said loudly to drive home my point.

"Alexa doesn't need a hearing aid. You need an interpreter," Sweetie replied with a chuckle.

"Hrrrumph." I snuffled. "I speak just fine, thank you. An interpreter is not needed for my enunciation."

We continued shopping without incident until Sweetie looked at me with mirth on her face and said, "Well, now we need some 'Cons and Minions.' Where might those be, dear?"

"I. DID. NOT. SAY. ANYTHING. ABOUT. MINIONS!" I screeched.

"Well, it's right here in the snack section." She was chuckling out loud now.

"Hush and let me see that list," I demanded with a hiss. I went down the rest of the items on the list and noticed that my Atkins M&M's weren't on there. How the heck did Alexa get "Cons and Minions" out of that? I slunk over to the shelf and grabbed them and threw them in the cart. Sweetie laughed harder.

The trip from aisle to aisle continued with me pouting a bit. Well, more than a little bit. I was pissed at Alexa. She was making a fool out of me. Stupid gadgets.

"Hun, when did you start buying your panties at the grocery store?" Tears were running down her face at this point.

"My what?" I asked.

"Your panties. See it says right here "Pant—"

"Give me that damn thing," I hissed as I grabbed her cell phone. Sure enough, right on the last line, it said PANTIES. What the hell were panties doing on my list? I don't even wear panties. Why would I tell Alexa to put them down? What was wrong with her? What was wrong with ME?

I was puzzling over the answer to the panties questions when I noticed that Sweetie was bent at the waist, holding her stomach and laughing out loud. Snot was running from her nose because she was giggling so hard. That in turn made me see the humor in the situation and I got the giggles too. I began to snigger so hard that I snorted, which made the laughter come even harder from the both of us. We looked like mad women standing in the aisle of the grocery store wiping snot and snorting. People began to gather and stare. We didn't care. We couldn't stop laughing.

Suddenly it hit me what *panties* translated to. "PEPSI," I screamed loudly. "Panties equal Pepsi."

The crowd of people started to shake their

heads and walk away like we were crazy or something. Imagine that! We were both laughing so hard that I sat down in the aisle as Sweetie, who was bent over, just laid her head on the handle of the cart and howled. We finally calmed enough to make our way to a grocery store attendant.

"Which aisle are the panties on?" I asked while biting my lip and holding my laughter to just a titter.

"Umm, panties, err, I am not sure that we carry that ma'am." His face turned bright red and his mouth made a capital O.

"Sure you do. I buy them here all the time," I said.

Sweetie fell over on the floor at the look on the poor boy's face. She was literally rolling on the floor laughing. That did it for me. I howled! The poor stock boy ran off. That just made it worse and we laughed harder…if that was possible. The manager came over to see if everything was all right. Sweetie and I composed ourselves enough to get my Pepsi and go to the checkout counter and pay. Only small sniggers erupted occasionally. We paid and headed to the car laughing again at the whole situation.

When we got home, Alexa and I had a serious talk. She had to learn Southern or I'd be damned if I ever went to the grocery store again. Sweetie could go all by herself, or better yet, she could take Alexa. That'd sure serve her right.

Wally World Fantasies
or
Alexa Part Two

"The odds of going to the store for just a loaf of bread and coming out with only a loaf of bread are three billion to one."
~ Erma Bombeck

Sweetie and I seem to be having trouble with remembering things lately. This has nothing at all to do with our age and everything to do with the fact that we are both so smart that our brains are getting full. That being said, and despite her obvious comprehension flaws, we now use "Alexa" to keep most of our appointments, what times we are supposed to take our meds, and our shopping lists. Again, our brains are very, very full of smart shit.

We were at Wally World doing some shopping one Saturday morning with our Alexa list pulled up on Sweetie's phone. She handles the list as the brains of the operation and I am the cart pusher, a.k.a., the muscle! Things were going well. Shampoo, check. Soda, check. Oreos, check. (Okay, forget you saw that last one. We are following our diet. I swear.) Anyway, things were moving quickly and efficiently with the help of Alexa, except for the occasional stop for me to sample each type of grape. This makes Sweetie angry because she says that I am going to get E. coli or some other dreaded disease and die right there in the fruit aisle. Pssshhh. I haven't died yet and I've been sampling fruit from the produce department since I was a child.

Suddenly, Sweetie turned to me with a start and squeaked, "What the hell is 'Grandma Brown's Fantasy'?"

"I don't know. I'll play your silly game. What IS Grandma Brown's fantasy?" I asked.

Sweetie whispered through clenched teeth, "No, right here, it says 'Grandma Brown's Fantasy!'"

Well, needless to say, I was confused. Which is not unusual for me. I didn't even know who Grandma Brown was, much less what she may fantasize about. Also, Alexa and I still have not had a meeting of the Southern accent minds. So, all I could think to say was, "Well, you go on with your bad self, Grandma Brown."

Sweetie sighed loudly and rolled her eyes all the way back to her brain. And she accuses me of being overly dramatic. "Let's go look around the aisles and try to figure out what the hell this even means. It may be an important ingredient for a dinner recipe."

We walked all over Wally World, up and down each aisle looking for what Grandma Brown may be fantasizing about. Nothing that we looked at even came close to sounding anything like that.

Suddenly, I spotted Paul Newman's Dressing. I held it proudly above my head and yelled, "Look, Sweetie, I found it. It has to be Paul Newman's Dressing. I mean, he is kind of old. And, a grandma might just fantasize about him. This is it, Sweetie. I found her fantasy!"

Sweetie looked at me as if I'd grown three heads. Then I got The Look. You remember The Look from earlier, right?

I slowly sat the dressing back down since Sweetie looked a bit feral and like she did not believe that Grandma would fantasize about Paul Newman, and I backed away. We then began to say Grandma Brown's Fantasy in different accents and weird languages. Nothing! It just made no sense to us or sound like anything that we'd ever used. We finally gave up and headed to the checkout to pay.

I had forgotten all about Grandma Brown or any of her fantasies on Monday morning when I went into the bathroom to get ready. I started putting on my makeup and began to giggle like a little girl. I giggled so hard and loudly that I actually peed myself. Sweetie heard me and came running to see what was wrong.

"I...figured...out...what...Grandma Browns... fantasy...is," I huffed through sobbing laughter. "It's 'Revlon Brow Fantasy.'" I held the nub of a pencil out toward Sweetie's eyeballs, and she simply turned and walked back out of the bathroom. I was not sure if it was because she didn't find the brow pencil funny or that she had noticed the spreading circle of pee on the floor. Oh well, what are you gonna do? When ya get the giggles, pee happens.

"Hey, Sweetie," I yelled behind her. "I still think Grandma Brown would prefer Paul Newman."

I hear Sweetie begin to hit her head slowly against the wall. *Thunk...thunk.* She really just has no sense of humor.

There Is A Proper Way To Do What???

"The lion and the calf shall lie down together, but the
calf won't get much sleep."
~ Woody Allen

Did you know that there was a proper way to get into bed? "Hrrrumph." Well, neither did I until Sweetie decided that I was doing it all wrong. Let me just tell you that I have gotten into bed the same way since I was a little girl. My momma didn't tell me any different, so in my mind, it was the right way. That is, until I met Sweetie.

Every single night she would giggle when I got into bed. Finally, one night, I asked her what the problem was. "Well, you sit down on the bed, swing your legs up, and oooch down like an inchworm to make your head hit the pillow."

"Yeah, so?" I replied.

"Well, that is not the proper way to get into bed. It takes you five minutes to get your head on your pillow and that is a waste of time." Remember, Sweetie is a touch (wink, wink) OCD.

"So, Miss Smarty-Pants, show me how to get into bed in a more timely and correct fashion." I was thinking that she was sleepy and would just laugh it off, stay in bed, and forget all about my getting-into-bed inadequacies. SHE. DID. NOT!

She popped out of bed like a jack-in-the-box,

told Alexa—that accent-challenged traitor—to turn on the lights in the bedroom, and took her place at the side of the bed.

"Okay, this is the proper way of getting into bed," she said. She then squatted a bit and leapt, then proceeded to do a jellyfish roll and hopped with a twist into the bed. Her head landed square on the pillow. I gave her a ten for creativity.

"There is no way that I am getting into bed like that! I will kill myself," I yelped.

"But it is the proper way," she said. "Just try it once. Come on, please. You'll never have to oooch like an inchworm again."

"NO...just no," I replied with vehemence.

"Puh-leese," she begged.

"Oh, alright," I agreed. "I will try it once. Then will you leave me alone?"

"Oh, yes, dear. I will," she promised. Whatever.

So, I rolled out of my oooched-down-into-comfort position and stood on the side of the bed. I was a bit afraid, but I was a cheerleader in high school. What could go wrong? Plenty. That's what.

I settled myself into the same position that Sweetie had started in—side to the bed, knees bent, head cocked to one side—and jumped. POW! I landed square on my ass on the floor. I looked like a jellyfish all right...a flattened one. Sweetie laughed. I glared at her from my position on the floor and said, "See? It does not work for everyone. I think my ass bone is broke."

"Oh, it is not," replied Sweetie with a giggle. "Try again. You just forgot to lurch toward the bed during your flip."

"Are you kidding me? Try again? Hrrrumph."

So, I did.

This time I landed on the bed. I was right in the same position that I usually ended up in bed when I did it my way, so I ooched down to my pillow and said, "There, I did it!"

"You did not do it. You ended up at the top of the bed and had to scoot (another word for oooch) down to get on your pillow. Epic fail. Try just one more time."

"NO!" I screeched.

"Please, baby. I just want you to do it right. I'm trying to help you," Sweetie pled.

"No way, no how," I said as I got out of bed to try it again. Hey, I was tired and my brain wasn't syncing with my words and intentions. I set myself into the proper position, prepared for takeoff, and jumped. I hit the bed all right. Straight into the headboard. I lifted my face, bloody nose and all, and stared directly into Sweetie's eyes. I then said the famous words that one usually utters when properly pissed off: "Bite me!" I ooched down into the bed, wiped the blood from my nose with the back of my hand, lay my head on my pillow, and snuggled up for a deep sleep. Jellyfish be damned. I would use my ooch-and-scooch method. Sweetie could use the flip-and-flop method all she wanted. I would use my way and be happy about it. Even if I was getting carpal tunnel from all the ooching and scooching. Sweetie's method be damned.

The Left Coast Lesbian Conference

"Sure, I could tell you I am no longer a lesbian or that I am no longer attracted to women and am straight, or I could even tell you the moon is made of cheese. I could tell you many things, but the moon will still not be made of cheese, and I will still not be attracted to men."
~ Cristina Marrero

Every year in Palm Springs, California, Sapphire Books holds a get-together called "The Left Coast Lesbian Conference." It is a fun time for us lesbians to gather and do our literary work and play and swim and such. It happens in the fall and is quite fun.

One of the years I went, we had a dinner at a nice restaurant. There were free drinks occasionally and I don't usually partake. This particular year I did, and I got lit up, snookered, blitzed. I felt no pain. You see, we got a drink ticket for one free drink and people kept giving me theirs. I think it was a conspiracy. They wanted to see me drunk. I just know it.

When we got back to the hotel, most of us decided that going swimming would be a grand idea. We all went and changed into our swimsuits, and since I was lit up, I was one of the last to get out to the pool. I had to figure out how to get my legs in my suit. It is very difficult, ya' know. Damn holes keep moving all around and once you get your legs in, you have to worry about pulling it up and getting your boobs to fit in the little cups. I decided that I either didn't need boobs or the little cups.

I walked sexily (read that: shit-faced) out to the pool area where I saw a bag of Goldfish. You know those little crackers that we force-feed our kids when they are little? Yeah, those. I decided that I must have some. I grabbed a handful and headed sloppily to the pool. Everyone else was already in there. I felt that I must enter the pool in a way that made me look sober. I didn't! I looked like a drunken skunk.

To make myself look better, I flipped the little skirt of my bathing suit. Liz McMullen let out a guffaw. I thought I was looking all sexy and stuff. Pffft! Then I dropped one of my snacks in the pool. How horrible! I was devastated. It would drown. Poor goldfish. I couldn't let it go down. I flung the rest of them onto the side of the pool and started flapping around like a fish out of water to get to the poor, lone fishy. Liz was leading the pool full of women in raucous laughter. I didn't see anything funny. Did they not know that the pitiful fish was submerged in the pool? It was dying and I was floundering to get to it. Couldn't they see that? Why wouldn't they help? They were all my friends.

I jumped up on the steps in order to dive back in, and gales of laughter burst forth. I was incensed. Why weren't they helping, and why were they laughing at me? "You farted," Liz snickered.

"I most certainly did not," I answered with as much self-assurance as I could muster. I was not positive that I didn't fart. I was too worried about my dear goldfish. Gales of laughter were echoing from the pool. How sweet. All my friends thought it was funny that *MAYBE* I farted, and they didn't seem to care at all about my sweet fishy now in pieces of dead goldfish floating in the water. Tears ran down my face. I noticed that they were running down my friends' faces too. Maybe they did care after all.

"Aww, thank you guys for caring about my sweet dead goldfish," I said.

"Your goldfish? We are not crying about your stupid old fish. That fart was tear-worthy!" Liz blurted.

"Screw you. Screw you all," I said as I huffed out of the pool and off to my room.

Giggles followed me to my room. I'd make them think that laughing at me was a good idea. I ran into the bathroom and grabbed my shaving cream. I'd get revenge on those biddies. I covered my head with a sheet from the bed so that I wasn't easily spotted, and headed out to their rooms to spray them down with the cream. Make fun of my poor dead pet goldfish. Hmmm, I'd teach them.

The Diverse New Job
A Totally True Text

Bubba: Hey Mom, guess what?

Me: You got your tongue pierced?

Bubba: What? What are you even talking about?

Me: Well, you told me to guess what and I guessed. Did I get it right? Do I get a prize?

Bubba: Seriously Mom, guess what?

Me: Well first tell me if Tate likes your new piercing. I hear that it can be really good for sex ya know.

Bubba: Good God Woman! I didn't pierce anything. I got a new job.

Me: Awww, man, I missed another one. I suck at guessing. But, now the job. That's awesome. More pay.

Bubba: Yeah, quite a bit more.

Me: Cool. Where at?

Bubba: A bit of a diverse company.

Me: Oh, is it a big company and what do they do?

Bubba: Oh, yeah, it's big all right.

Me: Tee-hee, that's what he said!

Bubba: Good grief Mom. What is it with you and sex talk today?

Me: Sorry, I'll be good ;) So, what is the company?Bubba: Well, the company is just like a shell company that owns the company that I actually work for. They are in MANY different countries. I can work from home. The benefits are great. It's a wonderful opportunity.

Me: Awesome. What kind of company are they?

Bubba: Well, therein lies the dilemma.

Me: Why? What dilemma?

Bubba: Well, their business is, shall we say, a bit out of the norm for me.

Me: Oh? Tell me more.

Bubba: Well, it's the largest online porn company in many countries...

Me: You're doing porn? That's why you get to work from home right? Cool!

Bubba: No, Mother, I am not doing porn. Lord have mercy!

Me: Well, it was an honest mistake. You said you were working FROM home FOR a large porn company making MORE money. What did you expect me to think?

Bubba: With you, I just never know what you'll think.

Me: Who all knows?

Bubba: Just you and Tate so far.

Me: Are you going to tell your father?Bubba: WHY WOULD I? I told you that we don't speak. If he can't accept me and Tate and our marriage, he's The Spawn of Satan. HE'S NOT MY FATHER.

Me: You sound like you're on a sleazy old talk show.

Bubba: Mom hush! Are you glad I got a new job doing Information Security for this new company?

Me: Bubba, I am so proud of you. You worked hard and are moving up the ladder. I knew you'd be successful at whatever you wanted to do. You have a husband, great kids, a home and a nice new job that you can do from home. Yes, I'm glad.

Bubba: Thanks Mom. ☒

Me: You're welcome son. I'll help out if you need new video content. I'm just not doing toe sucking videos. That's gross.

Bubba: Well, maybe I'll do those ;)

Me: K, love you, bye!

Bubba: Tee-hee.

When Is A Fly Not A Fly

"You catch a lot more flies with honey than vinegar, as they say, though I warrant you get even more flies with corpses. Flies aren't too picky, when you come to it."
~ Thomm Quackenbush

I recently got a phone call from Buddy. He sounded very forlorn, and it really worried me. You see, Buddy doesn't get forlorn. He is that glass-half-full kinda guy. But today, he was forlorn. Isn't forlorn a weird word? Say it out loud three times really fast. Strange word, right?

Anyway, Buddy sounded forlorn. "I need to ask you a question," he said forlornly. Ha, ha! Forlornly is even weirder than forlorn

Anyhow, I became frightened then. Something was wrong! I knew, just then, that he had forgotten to wear a condom during sex and now he had herpes or chlamydia or maybe even gonorrhea. Oh Lord! I had given all my kids "the talk." I had used books with really gross pictures, slide shows, and even taught them how to put a condom on a banana in the correct manner. (I taught sex education to teenage boys. Can ya tell?)

So, as I thought of all the dreaded diseases out there, I just asked him straight out, "Buddy, is it syphilis? Do you have sores on or around your penis?"

"Mom! No, I do not have sores anywhere near

my penis. Why would you even ask such a thing?" he asked loudly.

"Well, that's good. Rules that one out. Do you have pain when urinating, penile discharge, or swollen testicles?" I inquired worriedly.

He bellowed, "Mom, good grief! I do not have an STD, okay?"

Whew, then the banana thing worked. Good to know. I have a grandson that will need some enlightening instruction someday. Since I had obviously taught my boys so well, I could teach him, no problem! He's very smart, that Steven.

"Well, son, I can tell that you are upset. What is making you feel that way?" I was trying to use my very best Mom Voice here.

"Well, Mom," he said dejectedly. "I was cleaning up at the bar and there was this little fly on the ground."

"Okay…"

He took a few beats and then said so sadly, "Well, it couldn't fly."

"Huh," I grunted

"Well, Mom, the fly that was on the floor could not fly." I could feel the concern from him.

I wasn't sure what the poor sad boy needed from me. So I just sat there on the phone trying to find the right words to say to comfort him—or maybe even the fly.

"If a fly can't fly, then what is it?" he asked with anguish.

"Umm, a 'walk' would be my guess. It was walking, right?" I asked brightly.

"Well, yes, it was walking. I tried to help it fly. I scooped it up and gave it a little toss into the air," he wailed. "And it just flittered back down to the ground and sat there."

"Well, what did you do next?"

"I watched it walk."

"Have you been drinking?" I asked. "Because this sounds like a drinking thing to me."

"Mother," he yelped. "I am just concerned for the fly or, umm, walk or whatever it's called. What should I do?"

"Well, son, as with all wild things, you should set it free,"

He was actually tearing up now. I could hear it in his voice. "I can't just set it free. Something huge and scary will get it or maybe even eat it!"

"Well, Buddy," I said with the wonderful wisdom of a mother. "Leave it there in the bar. It's better to be a 'walk' than a 'dead.'"

"Mother, that's so mean," he wailed.

"It could be worse, son. You could have gonorrhea."

All Hail The Queen Of Lesbians

"I am not here to entertain straight people."
~ Sarah Schulman

Well, guess what happened to me a couple of weeks ago? Sweetie revoked my lesbian card! Can you believe that? She just yanked it out of my hand and ripped that sucker into a million little pieces while I watched, mouth agape. I was devastated. What had I truly done wrong? All I said is that I did not like Xena. Sweetie immediately went into a seizure-like state. Her eyes fluttered backward. She grew rigid. She began to shake. I was very, very afraid that this one little sentence had pushed her over the edge. She raised her right hand toward me and walked away in a zombie-like fashion.

I followed closely behind her to make sure she didn't fall. Her gait was seriously off-kilter and a wee bit scary. Once she reached the living room, I tried to make amends. She was having none of it, so I did the only thing that I could think of in order to get my lesbian card back. Manual labor. That should do it. I headed to the garage and grabbed the pressure washer. I thought if I washed the sidewalk and driveway to perfection, she would present me with a new card. Pressure washing is very lesbianish (yes, that's a word. I'm a writer. I know these things).

This pressure washing thing is not fun. Nor

easy. Why in the hell do lesbians like to do it? I started wrestling with the hose and got myself all tangled up. After jumping through hoops, literally, I grabbed the sprayer and turned that sucker on. It was like taming a copperhead. It flew this way, that way, up, down, washing me mostly. I finally got the hang of it...sort of...and was on my way. I was pressure washing. Me, the lesbian without a card. I'd show Sweetie. If it was the last thing that I did. And, at the rate I was going, it just might be. It took me forty-five minutes to finish one sidewalk paver and I was done. Done, I tell you. To my untrained eye, the section that I did looked barely different from the other sections. I, however, looked very different. My hair was hanging limply to my shoulders. Water was dripping from the ends. Every single inch of skin that was exposed was dripping with mud and my clothes looked like I had been rummaging through a landfill. It looked kind of like I had fought an octopus, underwater, fully clothed, and the octopus had inked me then kicked my ass. Done! I was done. If the paver I did looked barely different than the others, why the hell bother? So, I didn't. I put that sucker back in the garage where it belonged. It could stay in that spot forever as far as I was concerned.

  I slogged my way back into the house and announced loudly that I had pressure washed. I wanted my lesbian card back! Sweetie swept past me so fast that I spun like a top. All the goo flew off of me and onto the walls in the hallway. I was instantly dry. Meh. Now I wouldn't need a shower.

  After Sweetie made sure that her beloved pressure washer was not broken since I do tend to, umm... rearrange the makeup of her toys regularly (read that as tear up). She plopped down on the beautiful brown leather sofa that we had gone on a quest for. She sighed deeply and said, "Will you please, please just try and watch one episode of Xena with me?"

"Will you get me a new lesbian card?"

"If, and only if, you make it through one full episode with no talking or fiddling or touching stuff or any of the other irritating things that you tend to do when you are bored."

"Okay, I can do that," I promised with a very tiny crack in my voice.

She turned on the television. Xena filled the screen. Okay, she was pretty cute. I could do this. A fight scene popped up on the screen and Xena yelled at someone and then there was some screaming. I looked down and noticed that I had an ingrown toenail. I began to pick at it.

Sweetie paused the television, sighed loudly, and gave me The Look. I stopped with the toenail and redirected my attention to the television. Xena and Gabrielle were gazing at each other longingly. I giggled and gagged at the same time. My mind then started to wonder: if you giggled and gagged at the same time, would it be a gaggle? I let that simmer in my mind for a few minutes until I heard the sound of the remote hitting the entertainment center.

Sweetie bellowed, "No lesbian card for you!"

Forget Seinfeld's Soup Nazi. She was the Lesbian Card Nazi!

"Hrrruummppphh!"

She jumped up and went to get her precious pressure washer to finish what I had started.

"Well, la-dee-da!"

I slunk down into the sofa, picking at my hangnail, and my mind started to work on a surefire way to earn my lesbian card back. My son Buddy's best friend knew Gabrielle's real-life persona, Renee O'Connor, from Xena. My fingers flew over the face of my phone.

"Buddy, it's Momma. I need a huge favor. I need you to get Renee O'Connor's autograph for me or I am out of the lesbian club. Done. Over. Finis."

"Why, Mom? You have already gotten your toaster oven. What could you possibly done to get you kicked out of the 'sistahhood'?"

"I don't like Xena," I wailed.

"Huh? That's like a prerequisite for lesbianism? That alone can get you kicked out?" He queried.

"Yesssssss," I hissed. "Help me, please!"

"Well, Momma, it may be hard, but let me see what I can do."

A week later, a manila envelope arrived in the mail for me. I ripped that sucker open and there she was in full Gabrielle gear! On the picture was a very nice inscription especially for Sweetie.

I jumped up and down for, oh, I don't know, a good half hour. When the neighbors started to come out of their houses and looked worriedly at me, I skipped to the house with a huge grin on my face and joy in my heart. I would get my lesbian card back for sure now. No way she could refuse me after this. I just knew it.

Sweetie was standing in the kitchen when I bounced into the kitchen with my hands behind my back. She took one look at my maniacal grin and began to back slowly away as if I had a lizard or frog in my hand. (Hey, don't judge. My big ole butch wife hates "creepy crawlies" and I have to have some fun sometimes.) I didn't prolong her fear, though it would have been fun, and whipped the autographed picture from behind me. I placed it in her hands. Her eyes grew large as she read the inscription:

Sweetie,
Thank you for all of your support over the years. Fans like you make it all worthwhile.
Love,
Renee

Tears spilled down her face. She expelled little hiccuping sounds. She looked as if she might faint. She blanched. (By the way, blanching is not a good look for people. Try not to ever do it. Just saying.) I grew afraid. Has this been too much for her heart? I thought that we had worked hard to get that cholesterol down.

She began to drop to her knees. Then she bowed. SHE. BOWED. Holy shit! She had snapped. I watched as she held the signed picture in one hand reverently and reached for her wallet with the other. She drew out a card and pushed it toward me.

"Here. Here is your Lifetime Lesbian Card. It can never be revoked. All hail the queen of lesbians."

She then presented me with the card with a flourish. Tears ran down my face. I was officially a lesbian again. A lifetime lesbian!

"Thank you, Renee," I whispered under my breath. "Sorry that I don't like your show!"

Peanut Butter Cups Are Always Good. No Matter Where They Are Eaten!

"Without peanut butter, I might starve."
~ Judy Blume

One rainy afternoon, Sweetie and I decided to watch an action movie that had been on our "to watch" list for a long time. We settled in on the couch, holding hands because we are loving like that, with a big bowl of popcorn with butter and sodas between us. To be perfectly honest, we each had a peanut butter cup as well. Diet be damned! This was a special treat for us, and we were dang well gonna take advantage of it.

Sweetie clicked the channel button and the movie started. Excitement settled in. It was just like a date...until the phone rang. It was Sissy and she just wanted to jabber. I let her know that we were watching a very important movie. Then I just hung up.

We watched fifteen more minutes of the kick-ass movie and the phone rang again. It was Sissy... sigh...again. She had forgotten what she had called about in the first place. She needed to know if she could substitute flour for cornmeal in order to make cornbread. Well, no! Duh! I told her of course not. Flour was for biscuits and cornmeal was for cornbread.

She was just flabbergasted! She was making

homemade vegetable soup that simply must have cornbread to go with it. I told her that she was going to have to hop her little ass in the car and go get some cornmeal. She would not have cornbread by using flour. Flour was for biscuits. Then, I quickly hung up. The movie was at a pivotal point after all.

We immediately started the movie back up and the damn phone rang again. We paused the movie. Guess what? It was Sissy. Again! She started with, "It was really rude to hang up on me, Mom."

"We are watching a very good movie. Please go make dinner. Use flour for the cornbread. Just pour in a can of corn. How bad can it be?"

"Fine. But, hanging up on anyone, especially your daughter, is exceedingly rude," Sissy exclaimed.

I hung up!

Sweetie and I grabbed our peanut butter cups, hit play on the remote, and the damned doorbell rang! It was the next-door neighbor, Rob. He was selling fresh-caught lobster. Who could have imagined that there was so much one could learn about lobster and that it would take an hour to learn it?

I learned that live lobster, which is what he was selling, should be feisty (seriously, a feisty lobster?), not sluggish. They should feel heavy for their size. They should flail at you with their claws and their tails should curl, blah, blah, blah!

I so do not eat lobster and Sweetie didn't really want any either, but she bought seventeen just to make him get the hell out of there. I took them up and filled the bathtub with water, sprinkled some salt in there, and left them to swim.

Once again, we started our movie. We had pretty much forgotten what it was about but it was now the principle of the thing. Also, we had (cold) popcorn and peanut butter cups to eat. That was important! Very, very important. The ass-kicking of the movie started again. We ripped into our candy and…the phone rang! Again!

"What, Sissy?" I screeched.

But this time it was Bubba. I am not sure exactly what he had to say, except I did hear, "President… blah…blah. Vice President…blah. Doing great…blah. HE LOST! Whoop Whoop!"

I just let him vent…for FORTY-FIVE MINUTES I never got a word in edgewise. Did I mention that Bubba was a political science/history major? Well, he is. Politics is his thing, and lately that had been all we had heard about.

I glanced at Sweetie to see that she was lying in a puddle. It was quite a sight. My peanut butter cup was now melted in my hand. It began to run down my arm. I started to lick it off. All the way down to my elbow. Man, it was good. It would have been better had we been watching the movie, but what's a momma to do when her child calls?

I took another glance at Sweetie. Drool was running down her chin. She was cross-eyed. She really did look pretty pitiful.

Bubba talked some more until I began to pretend to choke on my soda. I acted as if I was hacking it up so that I needed to get off the phone before I died. Sue me for being a bit dramatic. I wanted my popcorn and the blob of chocolate that was still smeared on my chin from all the licking that I had already done. I really wanted the taste of the chocolate and peanut butter that was left.

Bubba did exactly what he always does. He's

such a good boy. He said, "Okay. Love you, bye."

No lead-up to it. Just, "I'm finished talking now." FORTY-FIVE MINUTES LATER! Why didn't I think of that tactic sooner? Sheesh!

I hung up the phone and glanced over at Sweetie. She was lying on the floor. Slobber was seeping from her mouth and pooling around her on the floor. I was afraid that she may drown, so I pulled her out of the puddle. She raised her head ever so slightly, and said in a heart-rending voice, "Do you realize that we have watched thirty-two minutes of a two-hour movie and it's taken us five hours to do so?"

Then her head smacked hard back on the floor, and I just knew that we weren't going to finish the movie that night. I licked the remaining peanut butter off of my chin and flipped the television to a game show while Sweetie took her nap. Or maybe she was unconscious. I was not really sure. Anyway, I figured she'd be okay, so I turned my attention back to the television and yelled, "Spin the wheel again. You may win a trip!"

The night was saved by a game show. Damn, I'm getting old! Wait, no I am not. I just think Vanna White is cute. Yeah, that's it. Never old!

I Have What On My Toe?

"I would sooner be Prime Minister of the moon than run another marathon. I've been really lucky; I didn't have any toenails fall off or anything disgusting like that. I still have three nipples."
~ Ryan Reynolds

While walking around the outdoor mall in our lovely little town in Florida a few weeks ago, Sweetie glanced downward toward my toes which were in flip-flops, cuz, you know, Florida. She got a really strange look on her face. I thought she was going to throw up and immediately thought that it might have been the lunch that she ate from the food court. I told her not to eat the lo mein. A burger was, after all, always the best choice. Any fool knows that, for heaven's sake.

I glanced at Sweetie again as I was really worried about her. She was bent over with her eyes three inches from my right big toe. I thought that she was going to faint, so I grabbed her shoulders in order to keep her upright.

"What's wrong, Sweetie? Are you sick? Going to faint, dying? It was the lo mein. I told you…" I was now blabbering incoherently.

"NO! It's not any of those things. There is a fungus under your toenail." Did I mention that Sweetie gets grossed out easily? No? Well, she does!

"Fungus? Are you serious right now?" I screeched loudly.

"Shhhh, someone will hear you and be grossed out. Of course, I'm serious. You have a fungus under your toenail. Gross!" she exclaimed.

I glanced down and saw a huge whitish mass under my right big toenail. What the hell?

"Gross! What is that?" I yelped.

"It's fungus!" she screamed. "How did you get that? How did you not notice it? I told you not to let the dog lick you. That's what caused it. You just never listen to me."

I was pretty grossed out by now, so I jerked out my phone to see what caused toenail fungus. How had I not noticed? Well, I knew the answer to that! I don't pay attention to shit. Just ask Sweetie. She'll tell you because that's what she's always telling me.

I scrolled through my phone search engine. Do you have any idea how many gross toenails there are in general? Well, you should look it up. Make sure that you look at the fungusy ones. Gah! Mine didn't look that bad. I didn't think so anyway. I quickly switched off the images section. I had enough of looking at those.

I looked to see if dogs licking your toes could cause toenail fungus. Well, it could not. I was right. At least on that point. Hrrruummppphh! Sweetie was wrong, which doesn't happen often according to her. Speaking of Sweetie, where was she? I looked up from perusing my phone and saw her vomiting into the bushes. Yuck! And she said that my toenails were gross. Vomiting is much worse.

I let her be. I don't do vomit. Not for anyone. Don't ask me to hold your hair back, be in the same room, or clean up after. Nope. Not happening.

I went back to my search engine and found that a well-known clinic says that toenail fungus is common. That's a good thing. I continued reading. Everything was fine until I read that one of the symptoms was "smelling slightly foul." Well, yuck, who wants stinky toenails? But, on the other hand, who was gonna be down there smelling them? That would just be weird.

I read on. "Most fungus is caused by yeast and mold." MOLD? What the actual hell? Now I not only had fungusy toenails, I had moldy toenails. Yuck!

Then I got to the part where the clinic said that it was "more common in older adults due to reduced blood flow and more years of exposure to fungi." How insulting. I felt my eyes glaze over. More common in "older adults." Excuse me? Older? Who were they to call me older? Bastards! I may be more…umm…more mature, but I sure ain't old.

I heard Sweetie wretch again. I did not respond… or care. Any age can vomit, but evidently "older adults" tend to get fungus-filled toenails. Older, shit! What could I do? Then I read VINEGAR! The article said to soak the afflicted toenail in vinegar. I could do that. I took off running to the store that sells whole foods to grab the biggest bottle that they had. Sweetie could just stay there and vomit all she wanted. No one would see it in the bushes anyway.

Unbeknownst to me, Sweetie noticed that I was running and started chasing me thinking that I had gone mad due to my fungus. She still had a bit of vomit on her chin, which made me grin so I said nothing. Let her be embarrassed. I sure was. Fungusy toenail. Gross!

I ran into the store and grabbed the biggest

bottle of white vinegar that they carried just as Sweetie caught up with me. She was huffing and puffing, puke on her chin still. I so did not care. I held the bottle of vinegar above my head triumphantly and let out a whoop. No more fungus...I hoped.

"I found it, Sweetie. The cure for toenail fu..."

Before I could get the rest of the words out of my mouth, she hit the doors of the store to get out in order to start dry heaving. Big ole sissy!

I went to the checkout counter and told the lady about my toenail fungus and how vinegar was the cure-all. She turned a weird greenish color as I pulled out my wallet and paid for my miracle cure. I headed to the door to go outside and saw Sweetie sitting on the sidewalk holding her head in her hands. She was muttering, "Gross...contagious...blah...blah...blah."

Didn't she know that I would now be cured of the fungus? Then a twinkle came to my eye. Hey, don't question me. I could feel the twinkle and it made me very happy. I walked over to Sweetie, who was still sitting on the sidewalk. She looked up at me with fear in her eyes. Evidently, she thought that fungus could jump. The look was all it took. I slid my fungusy toenail right up to hers and rubbed them together. She turned even paler than she was before and rose to push me away. I took off running with a huge grin on my face as I screamed at the top of my lungs, "Hey, Sweetie, there's a fungus among us!"

I was just far enough away to hear her hurl again.

Moral of the story: Even toenail fungus can be fun. Except for the "older" part. That sucks!

FLASHBACK
Who's Your Daddy?

"My kids always ask me which one of them is my favorite. I don't tell them that I really don't like any of them."
~ Anonymous

Once, while shopping at Wally World with my three biological children and two foster children, I noticed two older ladies following us from department to department. I knew what they were thinking due to the size of my town and the fact that the people there tended to be to be a wee bit racist as well as a tad homophobic. This is the reason that I got married and had children at a young age. That was what was expected of me. Anyhow, I simply chose to ignore the ladies. I figured that they would get bored chattering about us and simply move on to tittle-tattle about some other poor soul. This, however, was not to happen.

The old biddies continued to follow us while whispering loudly about my family. You see, my children have the same daddy yet they look very different. My oldest son is dark-haired with pale skin. The middle child, my daughter, is blond with tan skin, and my youngest son is a bright redhead with light skin. That alone was enough to make the busybodies prattle on about the fatherhood of my children as well as my reputation. Add all that to the fact that my foster daughters were both biracial, one black and white, one Samoan and white. I am a natural blonde…umm…yeah…that. This was normal to us. Them, not so much.

The ladies—and I use that term very loosely—were stage-whispering about us and it was very obvious.

"Whisper…blond hair…whisper, whisper…dark skin…whisper, whisper…well, we know what she's been doing…welfare."

I was trying very hard to be a good girl for a change because I didn't want to make a scene in front of the kids. The ladies continued following us and the whispers were now full-blown screeching.

"Floozy…must not work…"

Again, I chose to take the high road and I ignored them…well, I tried to. I know that's hard to believe isn't it? Me, being quiet.

The three big kids—which were my biological kids, and still are on most days…hee, hee—were getting antsy. They loved their sisters, biological or not. My oldest son, Bubba, was too polite to say anything. My daughter, Sissy, was scared. But my nine-year-old son, the redhead (of course!), was another matter. I noticed that the more that the ladies blathered rudely, the more Buddy twitched. I got nervous at this point. Buddy speaks his mind. What was I supposed to do? Slap my hand over his mouth? Shush him before he even started talking? Knock him unconscious? I am the momma. I should know these things.

Before I had the chance to make the choice to make the decision on what to do, (I was leaning toward knocking him unconscious), he turned around quickly and hitched up his britches which is Southern for "pulled up his pants to his underarms," stared the two old busybodies straight in the eyes, and bellowed, "Hey, you two. Yeah you. The nosy old biddies. Guess what? You can quit talking about us now. Yes, we all have different daddies. My mom is a 'ho' and just can't help herself when she sees a handsome man. No, she doesn't work and collects welfare. Does that answer all of your questions, or do you have more?"

One of the ladies fainted. The other paled to the color of snow.

I slapped my hand over Buddy's mouth, grabbed him by the ear, and dragged him away…quickly! Bubba, who was pushing the girls in the buggy, was hee-hawing. Sissy looked confused as if she were wondering if this was all true, which was pretty much normal for her. And Buddy looked mighty pleased with himself. The other two girls were too young to realize what the hell was going on, so they were just grinning as if this were all fun and games.

"What the hell was that?" I asked Buddy as we finally came to a stop far, far away from the nosy old ladies.

"It was fun, Momma. Lots of fun! Who are they to question our family anyway? Old busy bodies." He shouted the last part so loudly that everyone in the store was able to hear him.

I turned bright red, grabbed the girls out of the buggy, and left it sitting there. The older two were able to walk out by themselves. Buddy, I grabbed by the ear. We all ran from the store at top speed.

"Why are we the ones that are leaving, Momma?" Buddy asked. "Those old farts were the ones to blame."

"Buddy, don't say fart," I screeched.

Bubba snickered. I shut him up with a look. Sissy still looked confused. Ah, hell, who am I kidding. She was confused. Period.

Then I answered Buddy. "You have a point, son, and that point is valid. Those old bags were just being nosy, they can just eat…umm…dog food."

All the kids looked at me quizzically then burst out laughing. Our trip to Wally World was saved even though we bought nothing that was on our list. We still had a good laugh and, in my book, that was the most important thing.

My Pillow Smells Like What?

"Why does my pillow smell like maple syrup? I don't even eat waffles."
~ Anonymous

While making up the bed one morning, I noticed that one of Sweetie's pillows was in really bad shape. It was her favorite pillow and one that she had had for about seven years. That should tell you something! The pillow was now flat, the material was threadbare, and it smelled like maple syrup. That could not be good. I quickly ran down the stairs to grab my phone so that I could research the maple syrup smell thing.

I discovered that the maple syrup smell could be caused by diabetes. Holy shit! Diabetes? Could the pillow be giving my love diabetes? I wasn't taking any chances. I grabbed that pillow, ran to the kitchen, and shoved that sucker in the trash can. I figured that sleeping on it and inhaling the odors could only make things worse, right? I was saving Sweetie's life. I'm good like that.

When we went to bed that night, she noticed that I had bought her a new pillow to replace her old stinky one.

"Where is my pillow?" Sweetie screamed dramatically.

"Well, it was flat, threadbare, and smelled like

maple syrup. A pillow that smells like maple syrup could be a sign of diabetes, so I threw it away and bought you a new fluffier one that does not stink. Also, you have a doctor's appointment the day after tomorrow to check and see if you have diabetes. You have to fast, so don't eat anything after midnight tonight," I said with a smile on my face. I was taking care of Sweetie. Surely, she could see that. What a good wife I was.

"OH! MY! GOD! That was my favorite pillow. I've had it forever and it was all broken in. Why, oh why, would you get rid of it? How will I ever sleep now? I won't be able to. I just won't! I know it. Oh, and I am not fasting or going to the doctor. My pillow did not give me diabetes." She was still screaming, only louder!

"Well, honey, my search engine said that was true and I was just trying to care for you. I love you and want you to be as healthy as possible," I replied.

"But I love my pillow and I want it back…NOW! Where the hell is it?" she yelped loudly.

This whole scenario was not going the way that I had hoped it would. I was trying to save her life. Couldn't she see that?

"I said, where is my pillow? I've had it for years. It is broken in and comfortable. I will ask again, where is my damn pillow? I love it. I truly do." Sweetie went from yelling to whining.

I felt sorry for her but I did not want her to die from diabetes, so I ran down the stairs to the kitchen, grabbed her beloved pillow from the trash can, and headed toward the door to toss it into the big outdoor bin so that the garbage truck could pick it up tomorrow.

I didn't make it. Sweetie was blocking the door. I bobbed. She weaved. She grabbed for her beloved pillow. I thrust it above my head, held it there, and ran. I was going to save her life. She was not getting diabetes on my watch. Not happening. Nope!

Sweetie then grabbed the pillow and a tug-of-war ensued. Damn, she was strong. She yanked her pillow from my hands and took off running up the stairs triumphantly.

"This is my pillow. It is the only one that I can sleep on comfortably," she said victoriously.

I sprinted up the stairs behind her. I would not be defeated. Just as she started to push her cherished pillow into its case, I grabbed that sucker and took off to the bathroom to get the scissors. I proceeded to whack that nasty, diabetes-laden pillow into pieces. It fell on the floor into lumps. I felt victorious.

Sweetie zoomed into the bathroom just in time to see the pieces of pillow scatter to the ground. She fell upon them and started to try to piece them back together. Her plan did not work. I had won. I had saved Sweetie's life. What a great wife I was. Right? Huh? I really was. Really! If that was so, why was Sweetie lying on the floor trying to stuff the chunks of cut-up pillow back into the pillowcase. Did she not want to be healthy? Did she not understand that the maple syrupy smell was bad for her?

Tears flowed down her face. Her shoulders were shaking. She was sniffing the leftover pieces of pillow. I kind of felt sorry for her, but not sorry enough to keep her from fasting and going to the doctor. We needed to see what was going on with her after seven years of sniffing maple syrup. Big ole baby. After all, it was just a pillow that could be replaced. Sheesh!

Buddy's Got Talent
A Totally True Text Message

Buddy: Hi Momma. Guess what I'm doing?

Me: Well, a good guess would be juggling while walking on a tightrope.

Buddy: No, that was last week. This time I am simply leaving the Dol-pee Theater.

Me: Excuse me. The what?

Buddy: The Dol-pee Theater. You know where they film the Americans With Talent show?

Me: You mean the Dolby Theater?

Buddy: No Mom. It's been renamed the Dol-pee Theater.

Me: What? When? Why the hell...?

Buddy: Well...

Me: Oh God. I hate when you start a sentence with "Well."

Buddy: WELL, we were watching the taping of the show where people show their amazing talent and I had to pee. I told the security guard and he whispered that I couldn't leave my seat during taping.

Me: Umm...OK?!?

Buddy: So, Mom, I really had to go badly so I told him again. He got very nasty and said in an extremely loud whisper, "I TOLD YOU NO!" How rude was that?

Me: So what happened then? Did you get up and go anyway?

Buddy: Nope, I made a grown-ass decision...

Me: Oh, Lord have mercy!

Buddy: ...and I sat right there and peed in my seat!

Me: No you did not!

Buddy: Mom, I'm a grown-ass man making grown-ass decisions and he wouldn't let me leave my seat so, yes, I did.

Me: Like real pee.

Buddy: No mom. Fake pee...Yes, real pee.

Me: Then what did you do? Leave quickly?

Buddy: Nope. The security man said that I couldn't leave my seat, so I just sat there, in my own pee, and enjoyed the rest of the show. You told me that I should always follow the orders of someone in authority so I did.

Me: Nooooo...

Buddy: Yup I did. I'd love to see the face of the person that had to sit there after me.

Me: Well, maybe it will dry by the next show.

Buddy: Not a chance. There was another show being filmed right after the one we were at.

Me: Seriously?

Buddy: Bahahaha

Me: Good grief, son. Wasn't there another option that you could come up with?

Buddy: Not a one. It is the Dol-pee Theater after all...

Me: Disconnect

Snapped

"I always say 'morning' instead of 'good morning' because if it was a good morning, I'd still be asleep."
~ Anonymous

Well, hell, a couple of nights ago one of our neighbors thought that it would be a peachy time to shoot off some fireworks. No holidays, no celebrations, just fireworks. This is a big ole "NOPE" in our household. Fireworks scare the bejesus out of our fur babies. They both immediately ran to their safe space—the shower—in pure terror. It was almost 10:00 p.m. That is bedtime for me and Sweetie. (Don't be all judgey. You, too, will go to bed at 10:00 p.m. someday—if you don't already. So there.)

We spent the next half hour calming our doggie children enough to drag them out of the shower. We began to get ready for bed as the dogs cowered in the corner and stared at us pitifully. As soon as they saw the bed cover turn down, BAM, they jumped in. And plopped on my side. Yay. But I suppose that was only fair because I am a good little lesbian housewife and Sweetie did need her sleep more than I did. She had to get up early for work.

I wiggled into bed as far as I could go. I ended up with my ass hanging uncovered off the bed. I got as comfortable as possible and began my nightly ritual of trying my damnedest to actually go to sleep. Mr.

Bubby and Charlie were already snoring. Almost immediately, Sweetie joined them. I just continued to lie there with my ass freezing off.

Finally, I had had enough. I rolled over and glanced at the clock; it was 12:34. In the morning. For heaven's sake. I decided to get up and go sleep on the couch because I figured all of my wiggling was sure to awaken Sweetie and we just couldn't have that. Darling girl.

The dogs crawled out of the bed and followed me into the living room where they promptly got into a fight. Charlie had nipped Mr. Bubby's ankle (yes, dogs have ankles. Look it up!) and off they went. It was on. Hair flew everywhere. I literally threw myself into the middle of the melee in order to stop it. I got a nick to the wrist for my trouble. For some strange reason, this signaled to them that it was time to go outside to pee. I completely forgot that the alarm was set and opened the slider. Well, that woke the entire neighborhood up, except for Sweetie. She continued to snooze. I ran over to the alarm pad and somehow remembered the key code the very first time. Go me! It was now 2:00 a.m. and the dogs were outside frolicking. Life was just getting better. Not!

I begged, I pleaded, I cajoled, and finally got the dogs to come in at 2:42 a.m. I fell back onto the couch in exhaustion. Right onto the dogs who had crawled on the couch before me. They let out squeals that echoed throughout the house. I sprang from the couch like a jack-in-the-box and ran over to peek in on Sweetie. No movement. Poor darling must have been exhausted from sitting in front of the computer all day.

Things were great until about 4:30 a.m. My

tummy started to rumble. Seriously? Sweetie needed her sleep and I rarely ever pooped, but I knew that I was about to make lots of noise doing just that! I hopped heel to toe to the bathroom clenching my butt cheeks together with my hands. Tears running down my face, I made it just in time.

"Ahhhoooww." I let out a loud moan.

"Arrrggggooo." Another followed.

Just then, I heard the *click-click* of Charlie opening the door. He's a smart one, that dog of mine, and he had figured out if he stood on his back feet and pawed on the door handle with his front, he could open the door. And he did so. I now had two dogs staring at me as I shat my colon out. I just knew that Sweetie had heard my groans. Surely this had woken her.

I crept quietly back into the living room. No one was awake. I began to think that she was just in a deep meditative sleep when BAM! I slammed right into the coffee table with my shins. I put my hand over my mouth to keep from squealing as I fell back onto the couch, rocking back and forth holding my shins. That's when I caught a glimpse of the clock and realized that it was 5:13 a.m.

Good Lord, Sweetie never sleeps past five. Oh my God. She was dead. She had had a heart attack while I was trying to let her sleep! I ran into the kitchen and grabbed a knife and hurried back to the bedroom. I stuck the knife under her nose to see if she was breathing. I was petrified.

Abruptly, she sat straight up in the bed and grabbed my wrist while at the same time doing some kind of fancy kung fu type of move and grabbed the knife right out of my hand.

"What the hell are you doing? Are you trying to kill me?" she bellowed. "You watch enough *Snapped* on television. You are aware that the spouse is always the first suspect!"

"No, I'm not trying to kill you," I yelled back at her for some reason. "I thought you had died because we were so loud tonight. I was looking for signs of breath."

"I'm not fucking dead. I was sleeping. Quite well actually. It was a quiet night and I just slept a little later than usual. No biggie. It was all great until you tried to stab me!"

Quiet night my ass! Little did she know. And, besides, I do watch *Snapped* a lot. If I had wanted to kill her, I certainly wouldn't have used a butter knife. Did she think I was stupid? I shuffled off toward my side of the bed, cursing under my breath, to finally get some sleep.

Excuse Me, We're Doing What?

"When someone says, 'expect the unexpected,' slap them in the face and say, 'You didn't expect that did you?'"
~ Unknown

Sweetie woke me up one morning and said, "Hey, hun, let's go for a ride."

Well, I had just opened my eyes at the screech of her voice and was a wee bit grumpy. I wanted to go back to sleep. Ride hell. Where could we possibly be going at 7:00 a.m.?

"What, where, are you crazy? It is seven o'clock in the morning. Nothing is open. Nothing is worth seeing. I can't buy shoes. What on earth is your problem?" Then I turned back over, covered my head with the pillow, and tried to go back to sleep.

"But, hun, this is very, very important. We have talked about this in the past. Well, the very past, past. You'll be happy. Come on. Get dressed."

She was so excited, and this in itself was unusual, so I dragged out of bed and pulled on some clothes. They didn't match but I really didn't care. Who in the world would care if a tie-dyed pink shirt and red shorts matched at seven o'clock? I slumped off to the bathroom and ran a brush through my hair, which stuck out on end even after the brushing. I then slapped on some makeup in clown fashion and announced that I was ready.

Sweetie looked nice and put together in her khaki shorts and grey T-shirt, which she vows is the normal lesbian attire (I still swear that those colors don't match, though!). Her hair was laying perfectly. She does NOT wear makeup. She threw an apple in my general direction for breakfast and we headed out the door.

She was giddy. This scared me. Sweetie does not do giddy. Except when it comes to Free Shredding Day (see previous story above). Other than that, no giddy! Ever. So, I was truly frightened. Where the hell was she taking me? Was she finally going to kill me as she had threatened to do on many occasions? Where would she bury me? Maybe I should have dressed more nicely so when someone found me, they wouldn't think I was a clown. Oh, I hate clowns. Why did I bring them up again? Now they are on my mind. Shit!

Back to the story. We jumped in the car and headed out. She turned toward the interstate. What the hell? Oh Lordy, I was really going to my death. We were heading in the direction of some Everglades. I looked like a ragamuffin.

"Sweetie, turn around. NOW!" I screeched.

"Why? Are you sick? Do not puke in my car. Gross!" she bellowed.

"No, I am not sick. I must change clothes and fix my makeup. If you are going to kill me, I have to look presentable for whoever finds me."

"What the actual fuck are you yammering about?" she asked in a voice that I can't even begin to describe.

"Just take me back home. We are not far. I must change."

"Oh, for heaven's sake. I'm not going to kill you." Then she glanced over at me and really looked at the state I was in and turned the car around. Quickly. I guess I really did look like a scary clown...but aren't all clowns scary or is it just me that feels that way? Oh well, I'm right anyway. Y'all know nothing if you think that clowns are normal.

We headed back toward home and when we arrived, I jumped up and ran in the house while she waited in the car tapping her foot impatiently. I grabbed a pair of flowing white pants and a flowered off-the-shoulder shirt and threw them on quickly. I then ran to the bathroom to actually comb the knots out of my hair and coif it into a nice style. I also fixed my makeup into a high-fashion style. I was ready. If I was truly eliminated, at least I'd look stylish when I was discovered. I ran back to the car, jumped in, and announced that I was ready to go to my death.

"Oh, for Pete's sake, I told you that I was not going to kill you. This is a good thing. I promise."

I was awake by that time and feeling giddy myself now that I knew that I was going to live and looked nice. Maybe it was the zoo or a butterfly sanctuary. Sweetie turned onto the interstate. It was in the direction of the zoo. Oh, goody. I love giraffes. They are so different from clowns. Damn, there it is with the clowns again!

Sweetie was grinning from ear to ear as we zoomed past the exit for the zoo. What were we doing? With the giddiness, the grinning, and the fact that she'd passed the zoo, had she gone truly mad? Oh, Lordy, something else to worry about. I was in the car with a madwoman and she was taking me to parts unknown. I leaned back and tried to enjoy the view.

What could I do now? I was trapped in the car.

After about an hour, we pulled off the interstate at a place lovingly known as Pizzle for some godforsaken reason. What were we doing here? There was nothing in this part of town except a grocery store, a chain retailer, and a home repair store (of course). She made a left and her grin spread to a maniacal size. Dear sweet baby Jesus, what was going on?

"Umm, dear, where are we going? There is nothing out here."

Then I laid eyes on a covered bridge over the water as well as a clapboard building with a giant steeple atop it. Where had this been? Why didn't we know that it was here? It was like a fairy tale. We continued on this route, with my mouth agape at the beauty, until we came to a traffic circle. Now, that was new.

Sweetie looked at me and asked, "How does one navigate these things?"

"I have no idea. Just get in the center circle and surely it will come to you." I had faith in her abilities. Mine, not so much.

Well, we went around that inner circle six times before Sweetie said, "Screw this. I'm going." She cut off a few cars that were in the outer part of the circle, but, what the hell. We made it, only clipping one car.

"Close your eyes. It is a surprise as I said. You are going to love it! I promise," she replied sweetly.

Now she was grinning maniacally, making me close my eyes and being very, very sweet. She was going to feed me to an alligator. That was it. She wasn't going to murder me. The alligator was. She was just gonna give me a good, hard push. I held my breath and closed my eyes.

"Open your eyes, baby. We're here!" she shouted excitedly. This scared the shit out of me and my eyes flew open. There, before me, was one of the prettiest houses that I had ever seen. It truly belonged in this fairy-tale village that was as pretty as a picture.

"Whose house is this? I didn't know we were going to visit someone. Why are we going to visit someone? You don't visit," I exclaimed.

"We are going to look at this house. The price is great. The community is great. The house is great. Let's go!"

I looked around. We were in the middle of a lovely community. There were kids playing, people walking and riding their bicycles. Some waved. Some said, "Hi." They all smiled at us. What was going on? We were just an hour from our house and people were waving and smiling. That was different. What was wrong with them? Could they really be this friendly? I was not convinced. WAIT! We were going to look at this house? To buy? Yup, Sweetie had lost it. I began to drool a little bit in shock. This was all too nice. Like a story straight from a book. My kind of place. The drool increased. This time in a way that I hadn't felt in a long time. It was too good to be true.

"Well, c'mon. You can't stand out here, mouth agape with drool all day. Let's check this sucker out, babe," Sweetie said with enthusiasm.

We walked up to the door. I stopped Sweetie and asked if she was sure that she was telling me the truth.

"Yes, this is an open house. We are going to check it out. Don't you like it?" she asked with a bit of disappointment in her voice.

"Oh, yes, I love it. It's just too good. Too perfect. We can't aff—"

"Shush. Let me worry about that. Just give it a chance," she pleaded.

PLEADED! Sweetie does not plead. What was going on with this day? I was still asleep and dreaming. That was it. Damn, I knew this was too good to be true. Sweetie pinched me under the arm to get me moving just like my momma used to do. I was actually awake. This was real. Sweetie opened the door to the house. It was gorgeous. We entered into a foyer. Then the living room and kitchen. It was an open floor plan. This was what I had wanted.

This little man ran to us with some papers that gave the details of the house. My eyes were wide, my mouth agape. I started to wander through the beauty. Could this actually be ours? Naaaah. Sweetie was just screwing around with me. Not nice, Sweetie!

I continued to look at the paint colors and the layout and bedroom after bedroom after bedroom. Then I saw an office. Oh, the bookshelves that we could put in there to fill with my beloved books. Then, I went to the master bath and there was a tub that you could swim in. You may not know me, but that is my dream. I was sold. A huge bathtub was all it took for me. Then, reality set in.

This was too nice. Too perfect. Too much of what I wanted. Oh well, I would live. I walked back to Sweetie, who had been walking and perusing the property as well. She was now at the kitchen island speaking with the realtor. They were having a pretty intense conversation. I just knew that Sweetie was explaining that this was all too perfect and thanking the realtor for his time. Then I saw a piece of paper slide across the island counter. THERE. WERE. NUMBERS. ON. IT.

What the hell? Fear set in and I felt the drool start

to puddle at the sides of my mouth again. It started to run down my chin and I felt faint. Was Sweetie putting in an offer on this house? We hadn't even talked about it or looked at other houses or even discussed moving. The fear of the unknown grew, so I walked over to the island to see for sure what was happening.

I was right: Sweetie was making an offer! I began to twitch. Then shake. Then sweat and drool dripped from my chin. I was going down. There was no stopping it. PLOP! I hit the floor.

When I came to, Sweetie was shaking me and looked so pleased with herself. "I made an offer on this magnificent house, hun. Isn't that great?"

"Umm, errrrrrr, you did what?"

"I made an offer. It is the perfect house and the perfect neighborhood. Aren't you happy?" she asked excitedly.

"OOOOH..." My head slammed forward and banged on the kitchen island. I hit the floor again. I was going to have quite the headache if I didn't quit this fainting stuff.

After a minute...or ten...I raised my head slowly and screeched, "You made an offer on a house that we have looked at once and talked about none?"

"But your face looked so joyous..."

"Forget my face. It's the makeup. Now take that offer back."

"No. This is perfect. The offer stands. Get yourself to a standing position. NOW!"

That's when I noticed the realtor man. He looked petrified. I wiped the drool from my chin and offered a handshake. With the grossness that was dripping from my fingers, he politely declined and just nodded his head.

"She is just having a moment," I yelped. "She didn't mean to slide that paper over to you. It was done under duress. Surely that doesn't count. GIVE IT BACK!"

The realtor man jerked that paper up as if it would dissipate. "This is a legitimate offer," he squawked. He held it tightly. I tried to grab it. A tussle ensued until Sweetie stepped in.

"Give me the paper," she said with venom in her voice.

I ain't no fool. I let go. The realtor looked terrified. He let go as well. Sweetie grabbed the offer and smoothed the wrinkles out of it. She slid it back over to the realtor man and smiled...sort of. "Get back to me as soon as you know something."

She walked and I dragged myself back out to the car where she began to jabber. "Perfect place... beautiful house...plenty of room...two-car garage."

Why was she jabbering? That was my job. I jabbered. About nothing. All I wanted to do was see the giraffes at the zoo. I guess this was all too much for me. My eyes fluttered once again and out I went.

I awoke to her shaking my arm. Hard. "Wake up, hun. Wake up!"

"Wha...huh...what is happening? Are you okay? Did we wreck? Are we at the zoo?"

She screamed, "NO! None of that. Wait, the zoo? Why would you mention the zoo? Oh, never mind. We got the house. The lady that lives there accepted our offer. Isn't that awesome?"

"But the giraffes...oh, I mean that's wonderful. I think. We already have a house. Now we have two. What will we do with the other one?"

"Sell it, silly. That's how it works. You buy one,

you sell one. Simple."

"But now we will have two mortgages and two houses to care for. Aaaarrrgggghhh. This is not the way it is supposed to be done. You are supposed to sell one house THEN buy another. That is how it works."

"Nope, I have already been pre-approved. The house is ours. We are moving, baby!"

I began to stammer. "You were pre-approved? When...what...where...you didn't tell me. Am I in the fucking twilight zone? Where are the giraffes?"

She answered patiently. "I don't know what the deal is with the giraffes, hun, but we own a beautiful new home in a beautiful new neighborhood. Aren't you happy?"

Then it dawned on me. We had a lovely new house in a place that looked like Snow White should be living there. I began to smile. I wondered if there would be talking birds or squirrels there. This would be a really great thing. I reached out and took her hand. "Thank you, Sweetie. You bought us a house in a fairy-tale land."

She squeezed my hand back and smiled. "You're welcome, hun. I'm glad that you came around and are happy."

"Just a couple of questions about the new house first, though. Where are the giraffes, and there are no creepy clowns anywhere around, right?"

Sweetie slammed her head on the steering wheel. I shut up, counted my blessings, and looked out the window quietly with my hands folded in my lap like a good, normal person. I began to think—which is usually pretty scary—we had a new house and Sweetie had made it all possible. She rocks! I smiled. She loves me.

Light It Up

A Totally True Text Message

Me: I'm so glad that you finished decorating the tree before you left for work. Thanks so very much dear.

Sweetie: You're welcome honey. I just wanted to help and I was up early and you were sleepi...

Me: I hear you. I see that you hung the Janeway ornament front and center...AGAIN!

Sweetie: Well, yeah. She has been on the tree for over 15 years and I know that you hate that ornament...but...

Me: And you added more lights I noticed.

Sweetie: Yes, yes I did. Don't they ALL look wonderful?

Me: NO! They do not. Who the hell lit up Janeway's crotch anyway?

Sweetie: Well, dear, that would be 7 of 9 ☒

Me: Thanks for the visual, Sweetie. Just thanks!

Tire Pressure

"La di da, oh what a gorgeous—KAPLOW!"
~ Anonymous

My eyes flew open with a start. Oh my... sheesh...hell...I had overslept and I had to go to see my psychiatrist in order to get my meds. It was a sixty-mile drive just to get there. I was going to be late. Oh, I was gonna be in trouble. Dominique, at the front desk, was a bit of a drill sergeant and was very scary. Should I just call in sick? Nope. Doc would just think that I was depressed and add more meds to my already impressive list. I threw back the cover and jumped out of bed, then ran to my closet and threw on a tie-dyed T-shirt and a pair of striped shorts. Don't judge. It was lying on the floor and I didn't have time to find matchy-match clothes. I could not piss Dominique off. I grabbed my purse, kissed Sweetie...I think...ran out to the car, and sped off at an alarming rate. This speed lasted for about three minutes. That's when I hit the traffic circle and a little old lady in a Buick that didn't understand traffic circles. She was going round and round very slowly. I couldn't get out of the circle without hitting her, which was becoming a distinct possibility. Finally, after about our fifth trip around the sun, I honked, which scared the little ole woman into stopping and I sped quickly around her and exited. I hit the gas. Being late was looking more and more like a possibility. Dominique was going to kill me.

I sped toward the highway and entered quickly at the proper time. As I entered, the tire pressure light came on. It flashed like a demon's eyes coming out of my dashboard. I was on the interstate. There were no exits anywhere near me. I felt a panic attack coming on, thus the need to see my psychiatrist, and popped my last anti-anxiety pill. I then called Sweetie to tell her that if I had a blowout and wrecked, I wanted her to know that I loved her. She sighed deeply and told me that I'd be fine until I could get to a gas station. I did not believe her. Maybe she wanted me dead. This would be a good way to kill me. And, it would be my fault. I was the one that made her watch all the murder-death-kill shows with me. She had been taking notes. Hmmmm...Impressive.

I got off at the first exit that advertised a gas station and THERE WERE NONE! ANYWHERE! Oh, yay! I pulled out of the parking lot of a seedy hotel and slowly, so as not to blow up my tire, I got back on the highway. I decided to just chance it. I knew that there was a gas station right off the exit by the doctor's office. I turned the radio up loudly and sang really loudly for thirty-eight miles. Finally, I saw my exit. I sped off the highway at an alarming rate. Screeching into the gas station, I jumped out before I even came to a full stop. I grabbed my wallet as I looked for the price. It cost $3.00 for four minutes. Air is more than a soda and a peanut butter cup—which I NOW NEEDED! I dug through my wallet and finally found the right number of quarters. IT ONLY TOOK QUARTERS. Luckily, I am a bit of a hoarder when it comes to change...and receipts...pens...oh, you get it.

I jumped out of the car, plopped in the quarters, and went to my driver's side tire to begin filling it. I reached down to take the screwy cap thing off and could not budge it. I was losing time, so I went to the back tire and was able to get the cap thingy off, and filled the tire until the pressure machine dinged. This is a nice feature, I must say. I raced toward the other back tire and repeated with no problems. I followed with the passenger-side front tire. This was going well. I smiled as I went around to try the driver's side front tire again. The time was ticking down...19...18...17. I was struggling with the damn cap thing-a-ma-bob. Then, the air stopped. Damn. Well, I figured that I topped off three of the four tires and that equals 75%. Those are good odds. I jumped back in the car, cranked up, and peeled out of the gas station. I hadn't gone ten feet when the damn dashboard light lit up again. It was the one fucking tire that I couldn't get to that needed air.

I was at my doctor's office by this time, so I parked and went in praying that Dominique was at lunch or doing paperwork or anything besides sitting behind the desk scowling at me. My prayers were not answered. The scowl was there. I was in trouble. "You are two minutes late...have to wait...you'll learn..." she muttered toward me which was a bit scary.

I pulled myself up by my bootstraps (well, the sandal straps. I live on the face of the sun) and announced loudly to everyone in the office that "Lorraine Howell is here!"

Dominique looked at me as if I was crazy. Well, I was at a psychiatrist's office. If the shoe fits. They called me back quickly. Maybe I had scared Dominique. Tee-hee. Payback's a bitch. I was in and out, prescriptions in hand, within a matter of minutes. I had learned a lesson on how to get back quickly and not have Dominique yell at me.

I then headed back out to my car to go find air for the one tire that I couldn't get to earlier. There was another little gas station right near the office that had an air machine AND a big, burly man walking toward it. I whipped in the lot, jumped out, and screamed loudly, "Sir, can you please help me get the cap thingy off the tire. I must have air in that one tire right now." I was frantic.

He gave me a strange look, but walked over and bent down to help. He struggled with the cap for a while, which I must say gave me a bit of pleasure, but finally got it off. I thanked him profusely. Maybe I went over the top because he began to back away with his hands in the air. He was looking at me like I was nuts. Maybe he just saw the prescriptions on my front seat.

I began to dig in my wallet for quarters again. What is it with these machines and quarters? Sheesh! Dimes spend just as well. As I dug, the realization that I had used all of my quarters began to dawn on me. Then I remembered that Sweetie had told me to "Clean all that freaking change out of your wallet. You're never going to need more than two dollars anyway."

WRONG SWEETIE! The air was going to cost me another $3.00. I decided to use my debit card since I HAD NO MORE QUARTERS! The little machine was so tiny that I could barely swipe it. But, when I did, NOTHING HAPPENED. I inserted the card into the hole at the top and again, nothing happened. Then I noticed that there was a tiny green light blinking on the top but the writing beside it was too tiny to read. I had left my glasses at home. So, I laid my eye down on the machine and it said "Swipe card." I did. The little green light started blinking again so, once more, I laid my eye on top of the machine and it said "authorizing." This was good. Then the little light blinked again. Down went my head to read the new message. "Using Debit Card Costs $3.00."

Are you kidding me? It costs the same to use my card as it does to get air. That's some bullshit right there! The machine finally beeped, signaling that my card had cleared and I was able to fill the tire, which took approximately four seconds. This made me want a refund for the other three minutes and fifty-six seconds, but there was no one around that I could complain to. Then I saw the man that had unscrewed my cap thingy. I yelled across the parking lot at him, "Hey, do you need some air? I can't get a refund and there are three minutes left on the machine and I really want a soda and a peanut butter cup so I'll sell you the remaining air for those two things." He sort of blanched and yelled, "Nope, I'm good," as he ran across the parking lot. I shrugged. I guess he was in a hurry.

I jumped into the front seat and cranked the car up. I also said a prayer that this had worked. I cranked the car and the damned light blared again. I had filled all four tires. What the hell was the problem? I whipped back onto the road and gunned it. Just as I hit the interstate, the lights went off. That's when I remembered about air needing to pressurize and stuff. Duh! Oh well, now I just had to drive sixty miles home without a soda or a peanut butter cup. This was all too much pressure for me. I'd probably need different meds now and that would mean another long trip. Sigh!

I called Sweetie and told her to get my bicycle out so that I could ride some of my stress off when I got home. As I pulled in, I spotted it. My bicycle tire was FLAT! Are you freaking kidding me? I ran in the house, popped one of my new anti-anxiety pills, jumped under the covers, and screeched at Sweetie, "Bring me a damned soda and a peanut butter cup, and, by the way, you owe me nine dollars."

She did not argue. Simply did as she was told. Maybe she was scared of me or thought I needed my meds upped. Oh well, I love her anyway. Almost as much as the soda and peanut butter cup that I was about to enjoy. ⊠

The Old Lady And The Dog.
(Sweetie made me make this the title of the story. She thinks she's so funny. I do not.)

"You start out happy that you have no hips or boobs. All of a sudden you get them, and it feels sloppy. Then just when you start liking them, they start drooping."
~ Cindy Crawford

Well, as this is the last essay in the book, I suppose I should finally impart some wisdom on y'all. When one is walking one's twenty-five-pound dog in a gated community, one should always be safe. Right? That would be a big NOPE, Skippy. (By the way, who the hell is Skippy and why are people always calling others that? Anyway, back to the story at hand.)

While going on our nightly jaunt, my sweet loving Charlie was cantering along the sidewalk of our lovely community. We were all alone and the wind was whistling through the palm trees. Bunnies were frolicking in the yards. Florida was lovely at this time of night. I was wearing, well...my sleep clothing because it was dark and I thought no one would notice that I was in sleep shorts, a huge T-shirt, and was wearing NO BRA! Boy, was I wrong.

Charlie and I had strolled almost all the way to the common area so that he could do his business when suddenly, this dog that weighed about 200 pounds and could eat Charlie in one bite, came up from behind us unbeknownst to me. For some strange reason, Charlie hates this beautiful black Rottweiler. HATES HIM! I don't know why. He seems to be a very nice boy and never barks. He's just frighteningly huge.

SOOO, just as I began to step up on the curb, still not realizing that a beast was behind us, Charlie suddenly sensed that the Rotty was there. He whirled and twirled and did a freaking backflip in order to challenge the brute. This pulled his leash and my arm straight up, backward, and sideways around my body and through my legs. My body contorted into positions that I haven't been in since I was a cheerleader in high school. I went into a death spiral and down I went. HARD! Right onto the asphalt.

There was not one spot on my body that did not make contact with the ground. I splatted straight down onto the street. I raised my head and realized that we were not actually alone. There were three men across the street. Shit! Someone—several someones, actually—had witnessed my moment of shame.

One of the men zoomed over to me like the Flash, "Are you Okay?" he asked worriedly.

(NO, I AM LYING IN THE STREET. IN MY PAJAMAS. WITH NO BRA AND MY JUGS JIGGLING. AND, PEOPLE SAW THE WHOLE DAMN THING. I AM MOST CERTAINLY NOT OKAY!)

"Why, yes, thank you. I do believe that I'm just fine," I answered politely, and Charlie sauntered over to see what was going on. His movement yanked my leg up in the air as the leash was still around it. I may have broken my whole body but I had held tightly to the leash. Oh, no, I had busted my ass and everything else, but the dog was fine.

Mr. Buff Guy said, "Here, let me give you a hand." He pulled me into a sitting position, my tits tottering in the wind. Literally tottering. OH. MY. GOD!

At that point, a woman on a bicycle rolled up. She totally looked like a disgraced former prosecutor who had been indicted for bribery but found "not guilty" due to a technicality, and now had to settle for the title of "block captain" to feed her insatiable need for power. She snorted, "You really shouldn't walk your dog in flip-flops. See what can and DID happen? Hrrruummppphh!" And she rode off with a flick of her bobbed blond hair. (I mentally flipped her off here, but my fingers weren't properly working in order for me to really do it.)

The other two men had meandered over to help by that time. I don't know what happened to the Rottweiler and his walker. They just disappeared. Charlie sat down beside me and stared at me like I had done something really stupid. So judgmental! My boobs were still bobbing around as I noticed that every single neighbor nearby had heard the commotion and at least one from each house was standing in their doorway watching.

"Mavis, did you see that woman fall? She doesn't have a bra on..."

"Terry, come look at this lady in the street. I think she's in her pajamas...snicker."

"Harold, you better call the cops. Some woman is laying in the street, she must be drunk."

Damn. So much for no one seeing me in all my nighttime glory.

The guys helped me to a standing position. I thanked them and walked away with my knockers knocking and what little pride I had intact, dragging Charlie along behind me. I was mortified! I could hear the guys whispering bits and pieces behind my back as I walked away.

"... ya think... okay?"

"...no bra...hee, hee"

"I hope..."

I mustered up a wee bit of dignity and headed toward home. For the first time I noticed that I was limping just a bit and my toe hurt. I really didn't know the extent of damage to my body, but I did know that the damage to my ego was huge!

On the walk home, the air was still. No animals frolicked. The dark was overbearing. I *hurt* in every fiber of my being. Charlie sauntered at my side happily as if nothing had happened.

The closer that I got to home, the more I ached. Dear God, how far had we walked? It must have been eighteen miles at least. Finally, as I was about to give up, the house came into sight. I was now crawling, with Charlie dragging me.

As we made it to the door, I flopped on my belly and screeched, "Sweetie, help me. I fear I am broken!"

Sweetie came running from the kitchen and saw the blood. It was everywhere!

"What the hell happened to you? Did you get mugged? Is Charlie okay?"

"Charlie is just fine. Thanks for asking," I replied sarcastically. "He just broke my ego and my hooters hung in front of the neighbors and I'll never be able to go outside again and we walked eighteen miles," I wailed.

"Babe, you only walked a quarter of a mile, and we have to get you cleaned up. You've been hurt pretty badly."

I then glanced down at myself. There was blood everywhere. It was dripping from both knees and my shin as well as pouring from my left elbow. My right big toe was throbbing and sticking out at a very awkward angle. I also had a knot the size of a goose egg on the back of my head. Charlie looked at me sweetly. I growled at him. He ran and hid under the chair.

After Sweetie helped mop the blood off of me, the floor, and the doorframe (it really did look like a crime scene, which was way cool but not something I felt I should bring up to Sweetie, who was now taking this very, very seriously), I hobbled to the sofa and fell backward with my hand to my forehead. I believe this is called swooning. I was bandaged from head to toe, but what was still hurting most was my self-respect.

What would the neighbors think? Would they think I was just clumsy? High? Drunk? Or, perhaps and worst, just an old and feeble woman...which, by the way, I AM NOT! Dammit I am not old. Or feeble. No matter what my kids say. I made a decision right then and there that we must move. I couldn't face those people again. Yep, that was the solution.

"Sweetie, I'm going to need you to look for a new house for us. Preferably in the Pacific Northwest. We have to move," I demanded as I pulled myself to a sitting position.

"Excuse me? We have lived here for only a little over a year and this house is perfect. We are not moving. What the hell is wrong with you? Do you have a concussion? Should we go to the hospital?" She stomped away muttering, "...move...mumble, mumble...hit her head...mutter..."

I lay back on the sofa and sighed deeply. Such is

my life!

Moral of the story: When walking your dog, always wear a bra in order to keep the motion of your melons to a minimum.

Sub-moral of the story: The perfect wife, perfect home, and perfect neighborhood can't guarantee that you will never be embarrassed beyond belief— even if you are the Happy Lesbian Housewife.

Oh, and did I mention that I AM NEITHER OLD NOR FEEBLE! DAMMIT!

Reviews for The Happy Lesbian Housewife 2

"Buckle up, put your drinks down, trays in their upright position, and oh, a warning—you might want to use the little girls' room first because our Happy Lesbian Housewife is dishing out her hilarious slices of life once again, and I'm here for it!"
~Yvonne Heidt, author of Meet Me in The Middle and Paradigm.

"Lorraine has done it again! So relatable, so real, and so funny. She captures the human condition at its "finest" and presents it in a way that you can't help but laugh—at her stories, at yourself, at the world. Thanks, Lorraine. We can all use a good laugh!"
~Jennie McNulty, stand-up comic, actor, host of "Chat and GO with Jennie McNulty

"I needed this. Truly. After a year of a pandemic where there wasn't much levity or laughter, Lorraine dropped this nugget in my lap, and once again, gave me the gift of some great belly laughs. While I absolutely loved her first book, this one isn't just hysterical (like Lesbian Housewife), it is relevant, well written, sharp, and incredibly witty. Lorraine's writing style makes it feel as if she were an old friend catching you up on some of the more memorable moments of her life. So many times, I found myself laughing out loud. It takes a gifted writer to write humor. Not every writer can. Lorraine has that gift in spades, and it is one she shares with her readers in such a way that when you're finished reading the book, you'll want to start it again."
~Linda Kay Silva, author of the Delta Stevens and Echo Branson series.

IF YOU LIKED THIS BOOK...

Share a review with your friends or post a review on your favorite site like Amazon, Goodreads, Barnes and Noble, or anywhere you purchased the book. Or perhaps share a posting on your social media sites and help spread the word.

Join the Sapphire Newsletter and keep up with all your favorite authors.

Did we mention you get a free book for joining our team?

sign-up at - www.sapphirebooks.com

About the author

Lorraine Howell has 5 published works, including Goldie Award Finalist and Rainbow Award Honorable Mention Memoirs of the Happy Lesbian Housewife, you can't make this up seriously! under Lorraine Howell and Goldie award winning Finding Home and Finding Fire as Shelia Powell with Liz McMullen.

She began writing as a way to torture her longsuffering wife, Sweetie who she lives with in a lovely little town in South Florida. They are parents to three grown children, Bubba, Sissy, and Buddy as well as their fur babies, Charlie and Bubba. They are also grandparents to Lacie, Mikah, Grayson and Eli.

When Lorraine is not writing, she can be found painting rocks for the kids in her neighborhood, cancer centers and mental health centers to name a few.

Lorraine welcomes and responds to emails at Sheliapowellauthor@gmail.com

Check out Lorraine's other books

Finding Home – ISBN – 978-1-943353-04-0

Firestarter Kayla Cruise has been kicked out of another foster home, her twelfth, and she's back at the railroad tracks where she always finds solace. Surprisingly, a woman shows up there as an apparition, offering something Kayla had been longing for all her life, a forever home. Not just any home, Tia Keating runs a group home for teens with special gifts...gifts like the ones Kayla has spent years running from.

The problem is that when something feels like it is too good to be true, it usually is. Evil is stalking Kayla and her new family. The Darkness is putting her dream placement in jeopardy. It also threatens a burgeoning relationship that Kayla doesn't quite understand, as well as the only true family she has ever known.

With the help of Tia and the rest of the family, Kayla is going to fight back. The demons won't get to take away her happiness, not this time. Will this placement be her Lucky Thirteen or will The Darkness destroy Kayla's hope for a happily ever after?

Finding Fire - ISBN - 978-1-943353-71-2

Tia Keating's sister, Scarlett Weiss, shows up on her doorstep just after Tia's daughter Magnolia is kidnapped straight from her arms. The kidnapping sends Tia's house into an uproar. The continued unrest causes two of Tia's beloved foster children to run away once Tia's erratic behavior finally crosses the line.

Can Tia and her family find Magnolia and the runaways before their lives are ruined or will The Darkness win this time?

Only an epic battle will tell.

Becoming Me – A Metamorphosis – ISBN – 978-1-943353-51-4

"Becoming Me - A Metamorphosis" is a journey though the darkness and light of the human condition. It opens up discussions on deep and serious subject matters. It also speaks of the joy and love that we all seek. "Becoming Me, A Metamorphosis" is an in-depth, raw, gritty and complex look into the human psyche. It is a beautiful journey of healing. This collection of poems sways your heart into the world of reality while keeping your emotions on edge. The purpose of this book is to deliver a profound and meaningful message to you, the reader.

**Possible triggers

Memoirs of the Happy Lesbian Housewife: You can't make this stuff up. Seriously! – ISBN – 978-1-939062-69-7

"A heartwarming reflection written with humor, wit and just the right amount of sarcasm, Lorraine Howell's fun and conversational style reels you in. Sit back and laugh as she shares what makes her "The Happy Lesbian Housewife." Jennie McNulty, Comedian, Co-host of LA Talk Radio show "Cathy is In, The Cathy

DeBuono Show" and author of a weekly(ish) blog on Lesbian.com. With a partner named Sweetie, three grown children that are threatening to go into the witness protection program and a career as an adult entertainer, Lorraine Howell delivers a somber, no nonsense look at the difficulty of coming out late in life and how it has affected her poor, pitiful family... NOT! She really brings you a weight-loss book that guarantees that by simply reading her tome word for word, you will lose 25 pounds by the end. HA! Don't you wish? "Memoirs Of A Happy Lesbian Housewife - You Can't Make This Stuff Up. Seriously!" is truly a no-holds-barred, irreverent collection of stories looking at the late-blooming lesbian, Howell, and her hilarious take on life, love, friends, family and SEX! Nothing is off limits...Did we mention SEX? So hop on board and enjoy the ride. You will laugh and cry then laugh some more. Lorraine Howell's The Happy Lesbian Housewife, will not disappoint!

Other books by Sapphire Authors

Finding Faith - ISBN - 978-1-952270-16-1

Faith Fitzgerald thought that if she got an education and became a high-powered attorney in Manhattan, maybe—just maybe—she'd gain the attention and respect of her absentee father. Considering he was the only parent she had left after her mother's suicide when Faith was just a child, she thought that's what it would take.

She was wrong.

What she dreamed would be glamorous and satisfying turned out to be grueling and thankless. Since she wasn't willing to play the game between the sheets, she was forced to stay in the cubicle jungle doing all the heavy lifting while the men got the credit and the rewards.

Deciding she is done, Faith packs up and, with the flip of the bird to the rearview mirror, leaves New York and heads home to Colorado. She has nothing there: no job, nowhere to live, no relationship with her father. Truth is, she barely has a relationship with herself.

On the drive home, she finds herself in Wynter, a tiny mountain town at the foot of the Rockies. Looking more like it belongs in a made-for-TV Christmas movie than on the map, Faith is utterly enchanted. When she tries her luck and buys a raffle ticket at Pop's, Wynter's charming café, her prize is far more than meets the eye—or the heart.

Enter Wyatt, a feisty, sexy southerner and waitress at Pop's, who just happens to be married to a local sheriff's deputy. All is not as it appears with the All-American boy and his Georgia peach.

A colorful cast of unforgettable and charming characters will teach the jaded attorney that sometimes to find yourself all you have to do is go back to the basics...and have a little Faith.

Survival – ISBN – 978-1-952270-18-5

After surviving a school shooting, Mona Ouellet moves from Montreal to Peterborough, switches her PhD discipline from English Literature to Psychology, and tries to move on with her life. Unfortunately, her nightmares follow her—and so do a host of "bad men" who seem to appear around every corner to make her life difficult. Her only escape is to fall into her research completely, where she soon becomes obsessed with retelling true crime case studies and enamoured by a waitress at a local diner.

Kerri Reznik is a waitress by day and horror writer by night, where she turns elements of her two-month long captivity in the wilderness with her survivalist father into stories to scare others. Though over a decade has passed, Kerri is still haunted by her brother Lee's absence in her life and her inability to reconcile with it. She seeks camaraderie with Absalom Lincoln, a detective on Peterborough police's force, where the two bond over mysteries, both true and imagined.

As Kerri and Mona's connection becomes stronger, their past traumas begin to intertwine and both of their worst nightmares begin to evolve and intensify. Each character must struggle to negotiate how to live in a world where survival is never guaranteed, and even when it is possible, there is always a cost.

Keeping Secrets – ISBN – 978-1-952270-04-8

What would you do if, after finally finding the woman of your dreams, she suddenly leaves to fight in the Civil War?

It's 1863, and Elizabeth Hepscott has resigned herself to a life of monotonous boredom far from the battlefields as the wife of a Missouri rancher. Her fate changes when she travels with her brother to Kentucky to help him join the Union Army. On a whim, she poses as his little brother and is bullied into enlisting, as well. Reluctantly pulled into a new destiny, a lark decision quickly cascades into mortal danger.

While Elizabeth's life has made a drastic U-turn, Charlie Schweicher, heiress to a glass-making fortune, is still searching for the only thing money can't buy.

A chance encounter drastically changes everything for both of them. Will Charlie find the love she's longed for, or will the war take it all away?

My Home is on the Mountain - ISBN - 978-1-952270-40-6

You can make your life extraordinary, if you have the

courage.

Cecilia Howison, the rich and well-known daughter of a prominent East Tennessee family, appears to be the perfect Southern girl, cultured, gracious, virginal. The actual lesbian she is feels restless and ready for something new. She finds it in a high mountain meadow: a girl, wearing nothing but overalls, asleep beside a violin. Cecilia accepts the challenge.
Airey Fitch is the mainstay of her family's hard-scrabble hill farm. She has no love for the Howisons or any their kind, who now, in 1931, are evicting the mountain folk to create a new national park. Despite them, she will hang on, despite them, she will seek a life in music. When Cecilia offers to make that happen, Airey dares to trust her. And wonders at Cecilia's hold on her thoughts.

Cecilia understands all too clearly the risks she runs by wooing Airey Fitch but cannot stop, lured like a moth to Airey's flame. Airey wants more than the passion Cecilia gives her—wants her heart. But the world they live in forbids it, and Cecilia is faced with a choice that only love can make.

Thundering Pines – ISBN – 978-1-952270-58-1

Returning to her hometown was the last thing Brianna Goodwin wanted to do. She and her mom had left Flower Hills under a cloud of secrecy and shame when she was ten years old. Her life is different now. She has a high-powered career, a beautiful girlfriend, and a trendy life in Chicago.

Upon her estranged father's death, she reluctantly agrees to attend the reading of his will. It should be simple—settle his estate and return to her life in the city—but nothing has ever been simple when it comes to Donald Goodwin.

Dani Thorton, the down-to-earth manager of Thundering Pines, is confused when she's asked to attend the reading of the will of her longtime employer. She fears that her simple, although secluded life will be interrupted by the stylish daughter who breezes into town.

When a bombshell is revealed at the meeting, two women seemingly so different are thrust together. Maybe they'll discover they have more in common than they think.